SOMETHING

for NOTHING

SOMETHING
for NOTHING

THE ATTITUDE
THAT TURNS THE AMERICAN DREAM
INTO A SOCIAL NIGHTMARE

BRIAN TRACY

NELSON
BOOKS

An Imprint of Thomas Nelson

Published in Nashville, Tennessee, by Nelson Books, an imprint of Thomas Nelson. Nelson Books and Thomas Nelson are registered trademarks of HarperCollins Christian Publishing, Inc.

Thomas Nelson titles may be purchased in bulk for educational, business, fundraising, or sales promotional use. For information, please email SpecialMarkets@ThomasNelson.com.

ISBN 978-1-4002-4859-9 (TP)

Library of Congress Cataloging-in-Publication Data

Tracy, Brian.
Something for nothing : the all-consuming desire that turns the American dream into
   a social nightmare / Brian Tracy.
      p. cm.

ISBN 1-59555-038-0

   1. Social problems. 2. Self-reliance. 3. Power (Social sciences) 4. Entitlement
attitudes. 5. Welfare recipients–Psychology. 6. Public welfare–United States. I. Title.

HN28.T68 2005

302.5'40973—dc22   2005024471

Contents

*To my wonderful wife Barbara, who has encouraged me
to write this book for twenty-five years.*

*Without her continued inspiration, these ideas may never
have been made available to mankind.*

Acknowledgments

Many fine and wonderful people have contributed to this book, and many have given a lifetime to assure that these ideas would live and breathe and have an effect on mankind.

First and foremost is Ludwig von Mises, perhaps the greatest thinker of the twentieth century, whose commitment to liberty, freedom, and the ideals of the free society have had an impact that may have brought down the Iron Curtain and assured the blessings of liberty to more people than anyone else.

President Ronald Reagan said that he had read everything that von Mises had ever written. His student, Frederick von Hayek, won a Nobel Prize expounding the ideas of von Mises. His colleagues, Milton Friedman, George Stigler, and others received Nobel Prizes for their contributions, all of which were influenced by von Mises. Jack Kemp, the congressman largely responsible for the Kemp-Roth tax cuts that triggered the "Reagan Revolution" of the 1980s, and which made America the most prosperous country in the history of man, was a proud "von Misien."

In addition, I would like to thank my friends at Heritage Foundation, especially Bill Beach, who, with his colleagues at the Centre for Data Analysis, provided many of the statistics and proofs of the sometimes controversial statements that appear in *Something for Nothing*. They all turn out to be proven true, irrefutable facts.

Finally, I want to thank my daughter, Christina Tracy (now Stein), who carefully reviewed the manuscript and pointed out areas where more proof or corroboration was needed. Special thanks also to my friend Larry Stein, the father of my son-in-law Damon, who reviewed the entire manuscript from the point of view of an objective critic, and whose additions and insights proved to be invaluable.

Of course, I want to thank my editor, Joel Miller, who has been a stalwart supporter of this book, and his boss, David Dunham, who made the key decision to assure that this book saw the light of day.

To all of you, and to those unnamed, innumerable champions of individual freedom and personal liberty, I offer my heartfelt thanks for your input and ideas over the years.

Introduction
A Society in Crisis

"The worst day of a man's life is when he sits down and begins thinking about how he can get something for nothing."

—Thomas Jefferson

There is an emotional, economic, and sociological epidemic sweeping across America and the world today, destroying individuals, undermining societies, and threatening the future of civilization.

This epidemic is rooted in the out-of-control and insatiable demands of thousands and millions of people to get *something for nothing.* This morally and ethically fatal illness can be contracted by a person gradually, or all at once. It is invariably fatal to success, happiness, and prosperity. It is emotionally destructive and ultimately destroys the ability of the infected individual to accomplish anything worthwhile and lasting.

The *something for nothing* disease is like a cancer that can begin with a single cell, or a single opportunity to get "free money" in some way, and which then grows into a tumor. This tumor, or obsession with free money, soon metastasizes with the cancerous cells and spreads to every part of the patient's life.

The *something for nothing* illness is like a computer virus that gets out of control and eventually corrupts all the other programs, often destroying the hard drive of the individual and making him or her incapable of functioning normally in society or in personal relations. It actually becomes a form of mental illness.

An Incurable Illness

The *something for nothing* epidemic is like a bacterium for which there is almost no antibiotic and which mutates and changes rapidly into different and unpredictable forms. Once this bacterium gets out of control, the infected individual lives, breathes, and thinks continually about getting more and more for less and less, and ultimately something for nothing at all.

The *something for nothing* illness is like a form of *mental AIDS*, which eventually destroys the moral and ethical immune system, predisposing the individual to seek every conceivable way of acquiring money, position, power, respect, influence, and temporary success in ways that are harmful and ultimately destructive to the individual and to everyone around him.

The *something for nothing* epidemic—cancer, virus, or germ—usually starts in the greedy and avaricious nature of immoral people eager to enrich themselves at the expense of others. It is the driving force behind almost every form of unhappiness, corruption, criminality, and anti-social behavior. This obsession with free money is the root cause of wars, revolutions, robberies, scandals, and almost every type of individual, social, national, and international treachery.

Multiple Origins

This epidemic can also be triggered another way, arising from a false sense of "compassion" for those who appear to be less fortunate at the moment. This feeling of compassion, which usually makes the possessor feel morally superior to those that do not seem to share his concern in the same way, soon leads to the demand to use the power of government to expropriate wealth and income from those who have earned it to give to those who have not.

The *something for nothing* desire quickly becomes an addiction. Once a person has been led astray by the siren song of free money, no amount will ever satisfy him. No matter how much he gets, for himself or for others, he constantly wants more.

Like a drug addict, who must constantly take more and more of the narcotic to achieve the same physical sensation, the *something for nothing* addict, especially the recipient, must get ever-greater doses to stop from going into withdrawal and the often violent reactions that drug withdrawal, or *free money withdrawal*, can cause.

In the pages ahead, you will learn the causes and the cures for most of the social, political, and economic problems of the modern age. You will learn how to recognize and diagnose this terrible human and political virus and how to guard against catching it yourself. You will learn how to stop its spread into every area of our world. You will learn how to pull it out wherever it has taken root and how to destroy it quickly and efficiently.

My Search for Meaning

When I was a young man, I set off to see the world. I had read the admonition of Solomon from the Old Testament years before, and it had become my guiding star, *"With all thy getting, get understanding."*

Because I had almost no money, I worked my way across the Atlantic to Europe on a tramp freighter, made my way across France and Spain on a bicycle, drove across Africa in a Land Rover, and over the years journeyed by bus, truck, car, ferry, freighter, ocean liner, and eventually by air. I traveled and worked in ninety countries, all over North and South America, Europe, Africa, the Middle East, and Asia, including Russia and China, as well as Australia and New Zealand.

Introduction

I learned languages and smatterings of languages as I moved along. I studied history, culture, art, literature, and political economy. My goal was to "get understanding" of the world and the way the world works.

In the process of traveling and studying, I read thousands of books and articles and conversed with many thousands of people from every race, religion, culture, creed, and national group. Like a detective, I sought clues that would enable me to penetrate the mystery of human existence, especially the reasons for success and failure, happiness and unhappiness, prosperity and poverty.

Unified Field Theory

In science, from time immemorial, there has been the desire to discover a "unified field theory." This unifying principal would be a single and yet comprehensive idea that simultaneously unifies and explains all events and circumstances in a particular area. This was my goal as well.

Whereas physicists from Sir Isaac Newton to Albert Einstein and Neils Bohr sought to find the unifying principals that would explain physical events, I sought something even larger. My goal was to find the unifying field theory, or principal, that would explain human life and activity. I was looking for the foundation principles of behavior, organization, culture, civilization, political economy, and the causes of power and prosperity in the modern age.

Late one night, in a small motel room, a flashbulb went off in my mind. In a single instant, I saw the reasons for success and failure in life and society with absolute clarity. In that moment, everything I had learned fell into place. Expanding on this insight became a life-long project. Over the last thirty years I have invested thousands of additional hours in reading, research, and study to explicate and validate this insight. This book is the result and the explanation of my findings.

The Way Ahead

In the coming pages, I will share with you a complete and comprehensive way of viewing your world that will enable you to make sense of almost anything that happens, anywhere, involving anyone. Like learning basic mathematics, for the rest of your life you will be able to add, subtract, multiply, and divide, or its equivalent, in your ability to calculate and interpret what people do and why they behave in particular ways.

Each day, as you interact with people, read newspapers, listen to radio, or watch television, you will see the desire to get *something for nothing*, or as close to it as possible, in action. You will be able to quickly understand and interpret almost anything that is going on around you at a higher level than ever before.

The Outline of This Book

In Chapter One, you will learn the *seven fundamental elements of human nature* and why and how it is that people are *hardwired* to do the things they do and say the things they say.

In Chapter Two, you will learn the *seven basic needs, motivations, and desires* of all people, everywhere, at all times, and you will develop the ability to understand the behavior of everyone around you.

In Chapter Three, you will learn the *ABC Formula* that explains success and failure, victory and defeat, happiness and unhappiness, wealth, prosperity and poverty, and how to organize your life and world in such a way that you enjoy the very best of everything that is possible for you.

In Chapter Four, you will learn the critical importance of *character*, why it is the only antidote to the *something for noth-*

ing, how it works, and how to develop ever higher degrees of character in your own life and work.

In Chapter Five, you will gain an understanding of the current *dilemma* we face in America and the world, how we got here, and how we can move forward.

In Chapter Six, you will learn how and why *politicians and governments* are so quickly and easily corrupted by the *something for nothing* illness. You will learn why and how power and money become addictive drives that can poison and pollute the entire society if not kept under control.

In Chapter Seven, you will learn how the *something for nothing* principle applies to *business* and how its positive expression leads to continually better quality and lower prices for more and more people.

In Chapter Eight, you will learn how *something for nothing* applies to the *world of work* and to your career. You will learn how to harness the natural drives and energies of yourself and the people around you to accomplish more than you ever thought possible.

In Chapter Nine, you will learn the root causes of *crime and criminal behavior* and how these behaviors can be effectively discouraged. You will learn what you can do to contribute to the creation and maintenance of a more peaceful, law-abiding society.

In Chapter Ten, you will learn the destructive effects of *welfare and government entitlements* and how the Law of Perverse or Unintended Consequences in the handing out of free money leads to circumstances that are usually worse than if nothing had been done at all.

In Chapter Eleven, you will learn how to analyze and examine each important aspect of *modern society*, understand its functions and dysfunctions, and see clearly what needs to be done to increase the level of health, harmony, and cooperation among people and groups.

In Chapter Twelve, you will learn about *America's place in the world* and how the world outside our borders really works. You will learn about America's unique role in the world and how she can best fill that role.

In the conclusion and summary of *Something for Nothing*, you will learn what needs to be done to improve the quality of your life and the lives of everyone else in our society. You will learn a simple, effective method of analysis that will enable you, for the rest of your life, to see and understand the world as it really is, not as people wish it would be or could be.

This book will open your mind and heart to fully understanding the world you live in. It will give you insights, ideas, and perspectives that will enable you to function more effectively in an increasingly complex world and achieve more of your goals faster than you ever thought possible.

"You can never lose anything that really belongs to you,
and you can't keep that which belongs to someone else."

—Edgar Cayce

Chapter One

Why We Do the Things We Do

"Practice the Reality Principle; deal with the world as it is, not as you wish it would be."

— Jack Welch

Human beings are amazing! We have the ability to think, feel, reason, decide, change our minds, and accomplish extraordinary things. Unique among all creatures on earth, individuals have the ability to determine the course and direction of our own destinies and to change our futures. We can continually write and rewrite the scripts of our own lives. For us, all things are possible.

Your amazing brain has ten billion neurons, each of which is connected to as many as 20,000 others. This means the total number of mental connections, or thoughts you can think is ten million to the twenty thousandth power, a number greater than all the molecules in the known universe.

You have the ability to process enormous amounts of information, learn huge quantities of facts and data, and apply your mind to achieving health, happiness, harmony, prosperity, and a wonderful life for yourself and your family.

No Limits on Your Potential

Your true potential is only limited by your *imagination* and by your willingness and ability to be, do, and have all the things you can imagine for yourself. And since there are no limitations on what you can imagine, there are no limitations on what you can do with your life except those you impose on yourself.

You have the ability to set goals, make plans, learn almost any subject you need to learn, manage your time, communicate and negotiate with others, overcome obstacles, and win your own personal victories.

If you live in the United States, you are surrounded by unlimited opportunities, protected by the best legal system in the world, and guaranteed personal liberty and individual rights. You are living in the most affluent time in all of human history and in the richest and most powerful country of all time.

What Holds You Back

With all these advantages and blessings available to you and to others, why is it that so few people realize their full potential? Why is it that so many people, by their own admissions, are "leading lives of quiet desperation?"

Almost everything you are or ever will be can be traced back to human nature and the elements of human nature that predominate in the things you think, say, and do. Human nature can be a blessing or a curse, depending upon what parts of it you embrace and encourage and what parts of it you downplay and disregard.

There is both a "bright side" and a "dark side" of your nature, an angel and a devil. These two forces compete continually in your mind and heart for control of your thoughts, feelings, and actions. Fortunately, these elements are not fixed, but flexible.

You are always *free to choose*. The only thing in the world over which you have complete control is your thinking. Only you can choose and decide what thoughts to think and dwell upon. Your entire life today, in every respect, is the sum total of the choices and decisions you have made up until now. Since only you can make the choices and decisions affecting your life, you are completely *responsible* for everything you are and everything you become.

There are many characteristics and qualities that comprise what we call "human nature." These are fundamental, inborn, hard-wired, unchanging instincts possessed by all human beings going back into at least 6000 years of recorded history. The starting point of creating an unlimited future for yourself is for you to understand *who* you are and *how* you got to where you are today. Once you know these factors, you can move forward with greater confidence to create the future you desire.

An Economics Lesson

Sometimes I will start a business or sales seminar by conducting a brief quiz. I ask the audience if they would like to learn four years of university economics in *four* minutes. Almost everyone smiles, nods, and agrees.

I then begin by asking a series of questions. The first is, "If I could offer you a choice of jobs, both of which pay the same, but one is easy and the other is *difficult*, which one would you choose?"

When I ask for a show of hands, everyone raises their hand and chooses the easy job over the hard job.

"That's a good choice," I say. "It is normal and natural for you to choose an easier job over a harder job. In fact, it is almost impossible for a normal person to choose a harder way to accomplish a result when an easier way is available."

Life Is Precious

The most precious of all human commodities is life itself. Life is made up of the minutes, hours, and days of your existence. Life also consists of the amount of energy that you have to expend.

Because you think "economically" as all people do, you naturally strive to conserve the amount of time and energy you need to give in exchange for any element of your life.

The more time and energy you save in accomplishing one task, the more time and energy you have available to accomplish other tasks and achieve other goals. In other words, by choosing the easier route, you actually increase the amount of *life* that you have available for other things.

The result of this instinctive way of acting is that you are *lazy.* Everyone is lazy. It is a normal, natural human instinct. It is both healthy and helpful. It is the way you conserve energy.

Laziness in itself is neither good nor bad. It is only in the way that laziness is *demonstrated* that causes it to be defined as positive or negative.

The Bright Side

If laziness is demonstrated by finding faster, better, cheaper, easier ways to accomplish tasks and achieve goals, which is the motive force behind all advancement in human civilization, then laziness is a *good* thing. It is beneficial. It is helpful.

Laziness is the force that has driven all improvements in technology, manufacturing, production, agriculture, transportation, medicine, education, and every other field of human advancement. The natural tendency toward laziness, and toward reducing the amount of time and effort needed to accomplish a result, is a major contributor to the quality of life that is possible for you in the twenty-first century.

The Dark Side

However, laziness also has a "dark side." If people's natural laziness causes them to slack off, cut corners, avoid work, fail to complete tasks, waste time, start later and leave earlier, and generally contribute less to their jobs and families, then laziness is bad. Laziness is bad in this sense because it robs the potential of the individual who practices it. It diminishes his possibilities in the present and undermines his hopes for the future. Laziness expressed in a negative way will usually ruin a person's prospects for success and advancement.

But laziness, in and of itself, is *neutral*. It is neither good nor bad. It is only in the way that laziness is expressed that allows one to make a positive or negative judgment about it.

What Everyone Wants

The economics lesson continues. I then go on and ask the next question. "Imagine that I could offer you two different salaries for performing the same job, $10,000 per year or $100,000 per year. Which one would you choose?"

By a show of hands, everyone chooses the *higher* amount over the lower amount. Even if the difference was between a job paying $95,000 per year and $100,000 per year, if it were the same job, everyone would choose the higher amount.

Again, this is normal and natural. It is mentally impossible for a person to choose less when he could have more, all things considered. The desire for "more" is instinctive and hard-wired into the human brain. Even infants and children, in every culture, when given the choice between more or less, for example in the case of candy or dessert, will always choose *more*. No education or training is necessary.

I then go onto explain, "What this means is that everyone here is basically *greedy*. Every normal person prefers more to less throughout their lives, in virtually every situation."

How Do You Express Yourself?
Just as with laziness, greed is neither good nor bad. It is only in the way a person *manifests* their natural, instinctive greed that makes the action or behavior positive or negative.

The desire for *more* was the motivating force behind the work of Mother Teresa of Calcutta and her Missionaries of Charity. They constantly wanted to help more people.

Doctor Albert Schweitzer of Africa was greedy in the same way. Throughout his life, he constantly sought more resources so he could help even more African natives as a medical missionary.

If a person who wants more of the good things in life for himself and his family works longer hours, continually upgrades his skills, and continually offers to serve his customers with more of the things they want, this "greed" is positive and healthy. It leads to success, achievement, esteem, and respect in the community. It enables the individual and his family to enjoy a higher standard of living and a more exciting future. In this case, greed is *good*.

The Dark Side of Greed
The dark side of greed is what most people are familiar with. When people strive to get rewards without working, riches without contribution, recognition without achievement, or power without service, they are manifesting the dark side of greed. Whenever someone attempts to get *something for nothing*, in any area, they are manifesting the kind of greed that is harmful to the victim, and ultimately destructive to the practitioner.

When the entrepreneurial and creative energies of people

motivated by greed are directed and channeled into productive activities, greed becomes a powerful and positive social good. It drives people to innovate and create newer, better, faster, and cheaper ways to provide products and services for others.

Greed Is Neutral

Many politicians, demagogues, religious leaders, and well-meaning do-gooders are completely ignorant of the natural, normal, instinctive nature of greed. They attack those who strive to get more, especially business people who strive for more sales, more growth, and more profits, as inherently evil. By *demonizing* the normal and natural activities of people in business, they strive to create support for taxes to take away the money these people have earned and give it to others who have done nothing to earn these amounts.

Whenever someone accuses someone else of being "greedy," you can be sure of one thing: The person using the word in attacking another is either ignorant, dishonest, both, or greedy himself. Accusing someone of greed is the first step toward using the law to expropriate that person's money and usually with the intent to use that money in the best interest of the person advocating the theft.

Improvement Is the Goal

We continue with the economics lesson. "If I could offer you a job where you would have wonderful opportunities for growth and advancement or I could offer you a dead-end job with limited opportunities or job security, which would you choose?"

Again, everyone chooses the job with opportunities for promotion and advancement. Once again, this is normal and natural. All human action is aimed at an *improvement in conditions* of some kind. Everyone prefers to be better off rather than worse off. Everyone hopes for a better future rather than a worse future.

You always have a *choice*. You can either act or not act. You can either do something or do nothing. The only reason you will take action is because you anticipate being better off as a result. This is the foundation principle that explains virtually all human and economic activity.

Choices and Decisions

If you are confronted with a choice of two actions, you will always choose the action that you feel will leave you better off than the other. Whether or not you are correct in your choice, you will always choose *more* improvement over *less* improvement. But you will only act if you expect to improve your situation in some way.

What this means is everyone is *ambitious*. Everyone wants to be better off. Everyone wants to improve his or her situation. It is only in the way ambition is manifested that makes it either positive or negative.

If your ambition drives you to become a better person, do a better job, work harder, stay later, and contribute more, then ambition is a *good* thing. It serves your life. It guarantees your present and opens doors to your future. The more ambitious you are in a positive and constructive way, the more you will accomplish for yourself and your family. The more ambitious you are, the better life you can create for yourself. All successful people are ambitious.

In the past 25 years, I have given more than 3000 talks and seminars, and spoken to almost three million people in 25 countries. In questionnaires and surveys, I have sought for the *common denominator* of people who seek to improve themselves throughout their lives.

I finally concluded there is only one word to describe successful people: *hungry*. Successful people are hungry. They have an intense desire to be more, do more, and have more than they have ever had before. They want to improve their lives and they recognize that, *"your life only gets better when you get better."* They are ambitious, in a healthy, helpful way.

The Dark Side of Ambition

On the other hand, if a person's ambition leads him to engage in behaviors that are harmful to others by lying, cheating, deceiving, defrauding, or taking advantage of people, this form of ambition is negative and destructive.

There are two ways people manifest ambition in our society. The first is by serving and helping other people. The second is by using and abusing people for short-term personal benefit. The first is a positive manifestation of ambition, and the second is a negative manifestation. But ambition itself is a *neutral* word. It is neither good nor bad in itself.

Time is of the Essence

The fourth question I ask to round off this economics lesson is, "Now that you have chosen the easier job paying $100,000 per year, with opportunities for growth and advancement, if I could give you that amount in full on January 1 of the year, or December 31 of the year, which date would you choose?"

Again, everyone would choose to have the money on January 1 rather than December 31. This is normal and natural as well. Human beings prefer *earlier* to *later* in the satisfaction of any need or desire. One of the many reasons for this is obvious. It is the old saying, *"Better a bird in the hand than two in the bush."* The earlier you receive it, the less risk there is that you will not get it at all. Not only that, but you will be able to spend it sooner.

9

In almost every case, people prefer earlier to later. People do not like or want to wait. They want what they want right now. We say, in our fast-moving society, *instant gratification is no longer fast enough.* People who did not know they wanted something until this minute now want it immediately, if not sooner.

In other words, everyone is *impatient.* Everyone is in a hurry. Look at how insistent children are in demanding that they be given what they want immediately. And adults are just children with better excuses.

No Value Judgment Attached

The quality of *impatience* is neither good nor bad. It is simply a hard-wired category of human nature. If the desire to get things quickly motivates a person to create innovative products and services that satisfy customers faster, impatience is a good thing.

If people work harder and faster to accomplish the same result, so they can get more of the things they want, impatience is beneficial and advantageous.

On the other hand, the dark side of impatience is when people cut corners, compromise quality, and step over or upon other people to get the things they want faster than they are entitled to. When a person's impatience for rewards drives him to engage in illegal or harmful behaviors that hurt himself or others, then impatience is a negative manifestation of human nature.

Impatience can be good. The driving force of technological advancement for hundreds of years has been the desire to produce products and services, achieve goals, and get results *faster* than before. The primary advantage one technology has over another today is that the user can get a result faster with it than he could with a competing technology.

A Quick Summary

At this point, I summarize the economics lesson with the following conclusion: "We have now learned about the first four instinctive drives of human nature. What we know is that everyone is *lazy, greedy, ambitious, and impatient*. This applies to every person, everywhere, in all circumstances. These qualities are neither good nor bad in themselves. They are neutral.

The qualities of *laziness, greed, ambition, and impatience* apply to saints and sinners, consumers and producers, salespeople and customers, businesses and markets, politicians and bureaucrats, young and old, rich and poor, educated and uneducated. This is the way the world works. The smartest thing you can do in your interactions is to anticipate and expect that people will always be *lazy, greedy, ambitious, and impatient* in getting the things they want.

Many people are shocked and angry by this sweeping description of human nature. They vehemently deny that this is a description of themselves. They are reluctant to accept that others behave this way. But this description of the way people think and act is not an opinion; it is a fact. It is an honest and clear description of the basic driving forces of human nature.

Laws Work the Same at All Times

There are certain laws of nature, like gravity, that we have to take into consideration in everything we do. The Law of Gravity is not a personal opinion. It does not function depending upon whether or not you know about it or whether or not you believe in it. Gravity works all the time, everywhere, for everyone, under all conditions, without exception.

The laws of human nature are the same. We do not try to change the unchangeable. We may attempt to modify them in ourselves and others or direct them into positive channels, but intelligent people accept these inevitable and unavoidable characteristics and behaviors and take them into consideration in everything that they and others do and say.

Your Desire to Be Happy

In addition to these four instinctive drives, there are three more basic instincts that are hard-wired into the human psyche. They are also essential to understanding human nature and individual behavior. The next, number five, has to do with happiness. Aristotle wrote, "*The pursuit of happiness is the ultimate aim of all human activity.*"

Everything you do is an attempt to achieve your own happiness, or even *more* happiness than you already have. In 1895, Sigmund Freud described this as the "pleasure principle." This idea subsequently became the basis of modern psychology. He said every human action is an attempt to avoid pain and seek pleasure. You are continually attempting to move from discomfort to comfort. You continually seek ways to be better off rather than worse off. You continually strive to be *happy*.

Only You Can Decide

Here is the challenge. No one can decide for *anyone else* what will make him or her happy. Only you can decide for *yourself*. Only you can select the particular mixture and combination of ingredients that gives you pleasure at a particular time.

You are unique, special, and different in all the history of the world. There never has been, and never will be anyone *exactly* like you. There will never be anyone with your particular combination of tastes, desires, feelings, habits, experiences, likes, dislikes, hopes, and fears. What makes you the happiest will be different from that of any other person you ever meet.

Because you are such a complex person, with so many dimensions to your personality, the exact combination of ingredients that will make you happy changes continually, from day to day, hour to hour, and even from minute to minute. Happiness is a *moving target*. It is never fixed or final. And only *you* can decide, because only you can feel inside when you are truly happy.

Human Nature Is Fixed

The basic premise of communism in the twentieth century, which led to the deaths of more than 100 million people in wars, revolutions, executions, and famines, was that human nature could be changed. Those who espoused communism, especially communist leaders, were convinced they could decide for others the precise ingredients of happiness best for the people they ruled.

They acted on the premise that human nature was *malleable*, like soft clay, and that man could be shaped, forcefully if necessary, into a new type of person. This person would be transformed into their idea of what people *should be*, without their normal and natural human wants, needs, desires, fears, and compulsions.

The Totalitarian Temptation

Communism has now almost disappeared, totally discredited by those forced to live under it. Unfortunately, there are still people in Western society today with this "totalitarian temptation," primarily academics and politicians, who feel that they are somehow capable of deciding for others what is best for them. They feel that most people are not capable of choosing the correct combination of ingredients that will make them happy.

They simultaneously conclude that they, being *superior* somehow in intelligence and vision, are capable of making these decisions for "the masses." Every attempt to move in this direction is ultimately destined for failure because you cannot change human nature.

What Makes You Happy

Everything you do is aimed at achieving your own *personal* happiness. Even if, in the process of achieving your own happiness, you sacrifice greatly for others, your family or your fellow man, everything you do is still inherently *selfish*. Only you can decide for yourself. No one else can think for you, feel for you, taste for you, experience for you, or decide for you.

Everything you do is *selfish* in that you do it from the perspective of what gives you pleasure or pain, comfort or discomfort, satisfaction or dissatisfaction. You are selfish in that you are a unique, self-centered human being, capable of making your own decisions and choices. No one can decide for you what is best for you except yourself.

Selfishness Is No Sin

The quality of *selfishness* is neither good nor bad. It is simply a fact of human nature. *Rational selfishness* is what you practice when you engage in behaviors that are good for you and not harmful to anyone else. If your selfishness drives you to engage in socially productive and helpful activities so you can get more of the things that make you happy, then your selfishness is a positive benefit to society.

If your selfishness is short-sighted and indifferent to the well-being of others, you may engage in behaviors that give you pleasure or satisfaction in the short term but which lead to greater unhappiness and dissatisfaction in the long term, both for yourself and for others.

But selfishness itself is neither positive nor negative. It is only the way that you express your selfishness that makes it either good or bad.

You Are Unique

The sixth quality of human nature has to do with the fact that every person has an *ego.* The word "ego" from the Latin means "I am." Your self-concept, the way you think and feel about yourself, is the "master program" of your subconscious computer. Everything you do on the outside is guided and determined by the way you think and feel about yourself on the inside.

The most important part of your self-concept is your self-esteem. This is defined as *how much you like yourself.* Almost everything you do is aimed at either *increasing* your self-esteem, or *protecting* it from being diminished by other people and circumstances. Human beings strive toward self-esteem, self-respect, and personal happiness all their lives.

The second part of your self-concept is your *self-image.* This is made up of *three* elements: the way you see *yourself*, the way you think *others* see you, and the way you would *like* to be seen by others. Almost everything you do in your interactions with other people is guided by your self-image. You constantly strive to improve your self-image, especially the way others see you, in everything you do that involves other people.

Your feelings of self-esteem and self-worth are closely linked to how well your self-image is *supported* by the way others treat you. The greater the level of respect and esteem that you receive from others, the better you feel about yourself, the more you like yourself, and the happier you are.

Vanity, Vanity, All Is Vanity

What this means is that you are vain. You are concerned about the way you look and appear to others. You are concerned about what people say and think about you. You are concerned about earning and keeping the esteem and respect of the important people in your world. It has been said that *everything you do is to earn the respect of people who you respect, or at least to not lose their respect.*

Vanity is neither good nor bad. It is a fact of life. It is a normal and natural part of your human nature. It is the driving force behind all of the industries that produce clothing, fashion, cosmetics, jewelry, perfume, and every other factor that contributes to the way you appear on the outside or how others think about you. Vanity drives people to achieve material success so that they can drive bigger cars, live in better homes, go to nicer restaurants, and generally be respected and esteemed more by people in their social circle and community.

The Glue That Holds Society Together
A positive element of vanity is when you set high standards for yourself, for your manners and behavior, for your dress and appearance, for your communications and interactions with others. The most respected people in any social grouping are those people who are considerate and sensitive to the wants, needs, and opinions of others. They engage in positive, productive behaviors.

In the society pages of any newspaper you will see photographs of people in evening dress attending charity functions in support of good causes in the community. People pay enormous amounts of money and donate significant amounts of time to be seen in the company of other highly respected people in their social circles. In this sense, vanity is a good thing. It leads to a higher quality of life throughout society.

There is a dark side to vanity as well. If a person's vanity and desire for ego satisfaction cause him to behave in negative or harmful ways, then vanity becomes a *negative* quality.

Many people manifest their natural vanity in hurtful behaviors such as arrogance, conceit, rudeness, disrespect, and impatience with others. It is quite common for people who have worked hard to achieve success in different fields to become aloof and distant when they finally reach the top. It is said that *success does not change you; it merely makes you more of what you already are.* For some people, their vanity gets out of control.

An Uncertain World

The seventh quality of human nature that is inevitable and unavoidable is *ignorance*. No matter how smart or well educated you are it is impossible for you to know everything there is to know about *anything*. For example, you could be the most brilliant, experienced, and educated financial advisor on Wall Street. Yet within twenty-four hours, thousands of the facts and figures reflected in stock prices and market activities will change. You will have to work full time simply to keep abreast. You will never know everything. This is true in any field.

Sometimes I ask my audiences, "Is there anyone here who is a *know-it-all?*" Of course, no one raises his or her hand. It is not a compliment to be called a "know-it-all." But there is another reason: everyone knows it is impossible to know everything about *anything*.

We live in an *uncertain* world. Every action implies uncertainty or risk of some kind, even crossing an empty street. There are no guarantees that any act will achieve its aim because it is impossible to have perfect information in any area. The facts are constantly changing.

Today a doctor can specialize in a particular area of medicine, study in that field for decades and still not know all there is to know or all that is being discovered in his specialty. No lawyer knows all there is to know about his legal area of specialization.

No businessman knows everything about his market, competitors, and customers. There is no such thing as *perfect knowledge*.

The amount you know about anything is tiny compared to the vast amount you do not know. For this reason, no matter how intelligent or educated, everyone is ignorant to some degree.

Wrong Most of the Time

Because you are ignorant, which is neither good nor bad, every choice you make is a "best guess" among alternatives. According to experts, your decisions will be wrong or partially wrong 70 percent of the time, or more. Your life will be a continual series of mistakes and errors. Everything you do will be subject to the rule of *two steps forward and one step back*.

You will make progress and regress. You will succeed and fail. You will be up and down. You will have moments of triumph and moments of defeat. You will make good decisions and you will make bad decisions. You will be right and wrong continually. This process goes on all your life.

Never Stop Learning

Over time, if you continually learn and upgrade your levels of knowledge and skill, continually have experiences and learn from them, and continually focus and specialize in a few key areas, you will make *fewer* mistakes than you did at the beginning. But because you are inherently ignorant, because there are always countless factors you do not know or do not account for, you will always be taking risks and making mistakes.

The quality of ignorance is neither good nor bad. The smartest people of all are those who are overwhelmed with how *little* they know. The dumbest people in our society are the ones who are convinced they are smarter than anyone else.

The more you are *impressed* with your own ignorance, the more likely it is that you will remain open to new ideas and information that can help you make better choices and decisions. On the other hand, the more convinced you are of how smart you are, the more mistakes you are likely to make.

When your perception of your own personal ignorance drives you to continually improve and upgrade your knowledge and skills so you can get better at doing the things that are important to you, both at work and at home, then ignorance is a *positive*, helpful, life-enhancing quality.

If your ignorance blinds you to reality or causes you to be incapable of making good decisions, then it becomes a *negative*, hurtful quality.

The worst manifestation of ignorance is when a person makes mistakes but is too *vain* to admit them. This is why your willingness to admit that you *could* be wrong, even when you feel strongly about your point of view, is the mark of the superior intellect. The very fact that you are open to the *possibility* that your information may not be complete enables you to think better and more effectively in that situation.

Putting It All Together
This brings us to the "blinding flash of the obvious" that came to me many years ago. It was the realization that everyone is *lazy, greedy, ambitious, selfish, vain, impatient, and ignorant*, only for different things and in different ways. These qualities are as normal and as natural as breathing in and breathing out. They are permanently hard-wired and programmed into the mental and motivational structure of every individual.

These qualities cannot be permanently altered or eradicated. They can only be modified, channeled, and directed by creating incentives that encourage their expression in positive and helpful ways. They compose human nature. Therefore, every attempt to create a system, institution, or government in opposition to these qualities leads only to frustration, suppression, oppression, or tyranny.

This combination of qualities can be summarized in what I call the Expediency Factor: *"People continually strive to get the things they want the fastest and easiest way possible, with little or no concern for the secondary consequences of their behaviors."*

Various Reactions

When I have explained this E-Factor step by step to individuals or audiences, I have experienced various reactions. Most people smile, nod, and agree. They recognize that this explanation makes sense. Others, however, disagree, sometimes angrily. Occasionally they shout and swear. Some burst into tears. Others actually stand up and stomp out of the room. But, as Ronald Reagan once said, *"Facts are stubborn things."* Or as Winston Churchill said, *"The truth: you can twist it, turn it, and bend it out of shape. But at the end of the day, there it is."* The E-Factor is the unified field theory of human behavior for which learned people have sought for centuries.

If the E-Factor is the driving force of all of human activity, and what people want, especially in material or financial terms, is to get the very most, the fastest and easiest way possible, with little concern for secondary consequences, this means there is a natural human drive to get more and more for less and less. And the very least that you can pay for something you want is zero. Therefore, the ultimate goal of most people is to get *something for nothing.*

The Easy Way

In physics, the *Law of Least Resistance* is accepted as an unarguable explanation of natural phenomena. In human nature, it is unarguable as well. People follow the Path of Least Resistance to get more of what they want the fastest and easiest way possible. And the very least a person can possibly give or pay is nothing. Human nature is like *water*, which continually flows downhill by the Law of Gravity. Human nature, in the absence of personal restraint, flows downhill as well. Like water, it goes through every hole and crevice. It constantly seeks the lowest common denominator, the lowest price in terms of money or effort, to get the things it wants.

The most desirable goal in human nature is to get *something for nothing*. This is the ultimate aim of economic man. This is the highest possible achievement. The very thought of getting something for nothing motivates and drives people to behave in ways that are otherwise unexplainable. Sometimes, the idea of getting something for nothing makes people *crazy*.

You See It Everywhere

As an example of how quickly ordinary people respond to the chance of getting something for nothing, you could go and stand in the middle of a downtown plaza where businessmen and women are walking, talking, and passing through. Reach in your pocket, pull out a handful of 100 one-dollar bills and throw them in the air. Within seconds, the plaza will turn into a madhouse. Like piranhas descending on a bleeding animal in the Amazon River, people will come running, screaming, pushing, punching, and kicking from all directions to grasp at the fluttering one-dollar bills.

The desire to get *something for nothing* has run amok in our society. As I wrote in the introduction, it is the great cancer that is metastasizing and spreading to every area of social life, business, and government. It is the driving force behind most public policies, programs, and activities. It is the galvanizing force behind every demonstration and protest march. It is the organizing principle behind much of modern politics. The desire to get something for nothing is threatening to tear our society apart.

Simple Truths, Simple Conclusions

In his book *The Magus,* author John Fowles ends with this penetrating quote from T. S. Eliot's poem "Little Gidding," *"And the end of all our searching will be to return to the place where we began, and to recognize it for the first time."* By applying the E-Factor to the world around you, you recognize the way the world works, sometimes for the first time.

Don't accept this principle on faith. Think for yourself. There is a simple way for you to determine the truth of this or any statement or claim about human action or behavior. It is simply for you to ask yourself, *Is it true for me?*

When you hold up this question and contrast it against any claim that is made in your personal life or in the world around you, you will immediately have a tool to determine whether or not it is valid for others.

It is amazing how many people recommend and espouse policies, programs, and activities for other people that they would never dream of engaging in themselves. They think these wonderful-sounding ideas would be good for others, even though they know it would be unacceptable to themselves.

Love Thy Neighbor

Some will argue with this explanation of human nature and accuse me of being too harsh in my assessment. They will say I am using sweeping generalities to pass a negative judgment on mankind. They will suggest there are many examples of people who engage in behaviors that are not *lazy, greedy, selfish, ambitious, vain, ignorant, or impatient.*

Nothing in this argument changes the facts. The sun rises in the east and sets in the west. Things fall down rather than up. People are *expedient*—automatically, instinctively, reflexively— even the person who commits suicide or loses his life attempting to save the life of another is acting expediently. In retrospect, his behavior may not be rational or acceptable to someone else, but at the moment of acting, based on his personal worldview and judgment, that was what he felt was the best thing to do at that time. We will talk about this idea later in this book.

The Greatest Gift

Here is an important point. The greatest gift you can give another, especially a child or a spouse, is the gift of *unconditional love.* You love a person unconditionally to the degree to which you totally accept him or her with his or her strengths or weaknesses, without criticizing, condemning, complaining, or demanding they change and be something they are not.

The key to building high self-esteem in *children* is to lavish them with unconditional love as they grow up and throughout their lives. This doesn't mean you don't disagree with them or have arguments with them at times. But it does mean you never question their value or attack them as a person. You may disagree with a particular behavior, but your love is total and unconditional at all times, without exception.

Judge Not

By the same token, if you really care about other people, if you are a genuinely warm, compassionate, and loving human being, then you accept other people the way they are. You do not expect them to change, or demand they be other than what nature has made them to be. If you really care about others, you simply accept that they will behave expediently in everything they do. You will accept that everyone else, just like yourself, is *lazy, greedy, ambitious, selfish, vain, ignorant, and impatient.* You will not expect them to act differently, but you will instead alter your own behaviors accordingly.

As parents, you do not expect your young children to act other than expediently. You don't become angry or upset about this. Instead, you organize your children's lives in such a way that their natural tendencies toward expedient behavior are channeled and directed into positive and constructive activities. This is a large part of the responsibility of parenting right into the late teens.

The E-Factor Reigns Supreme

Let me recap this chapter by saying once more that people are *lazy, greedy, ambitious, selfish, vain, ignorant, and impatient.* They are expedient in their behaviors. They seek the path of least resistance. *They strive continually to get the things they want the fastest and easiest way possible, with little concern for the long-term consequences of their behaviors.* Above all, they want *something for nothing* or for as little effort or expense as they can get away with, whenever possible.

In Chapter Two, you will learn what it is that people driven by expediency want more than anything else, and in Chapter Three you will learn how they get it.

"Sooner or later, everyone sits down to a banquet of consequences."

— Robert Louis Stevenson

What We All Want

"Events are influenced by our very great desires."
— William James

We now know that people are *lazy, greedy, ambitious, selfish, vain, ignorant, and impatient,* that is, completely expedient and driven to choose the fastest and easiest way to get the things they want with little or no consideration for secondary consequences. We also know that the very least a person can give in exchange for anything is *nothing,* so people are continually striving to get something for nothing.

In marketing, the most powerful and popular word, in any language, in any advertisement, worldwide, is the word "free." The other popular words that grab attention, arouse desire, and stimulate buying activity are words like *easy, fast, improved, you, popular, tested,* and *proven.* These offers are completely consistent with the E-Factor.

Human Wants Are Unlimited
In a fast-changing world, people may want a thousand different things, constantly changing from minute to minute, hour to

hour, and day to day. The fact is that human wants are unlimited. The only limits on what a person can get are *external constraints,* the fact that he cannot afford them and there is no other way to get them except by earning them and paying for them.

In addition, a person may be restrained from the unlimited fulfillment of wants by *internal constraints.* The individual may decide personally to limit his appetites and desires and instead content himself with what he already has. Without *internal* constraints, people soon lose all control over themselves and their appetites.

You see this unlimited desire for "more" everywhere in the world around you. While his people starved and died for lack of food and medicine, Saddam Hussein built at least twenty-nine enormous palaces costing hundreds of millions of dollars and still wanted *more.* Wealthy business people, athletes, and movie stars often buy garages full of cars, multiple households and estates, homes in exotic locations, and every type of jewelry, clothing, and other toys. No amount is ever enough.

What Everyone Wants
Nonetheless, all human desires can be placed under one of *seven* different umbrellas. Everything that a person wants, however it is defined, can be included in one of these seven categories.

All human needs tend to be organized in a scale, from the most basic to the most refined. The pioneer in this area of human motivation and need satisfaction was psychologist Abraham Maslow. He postulated a "hierarchy of needs" that people attempted to satisfy in order, from the lowest to the highest.

The Hierarchy of Needs
In Maslow's hierarchy, the first and most basic need is *safety and*

survival, to preserve one's life. If for any reason your survival is threatened, staying alive will become the sole and central need and motivation of your life. Survival is the most powerful of all instinctual drives.

The second need in Maslow's hierarchy is *security*. This includes not only physical security but also financial and emotional security. Once your survival is assured, you turn naturally and automatically to achieving security in the important areas of your life. If your security is threatened for any reason, you immediately forget everything else in your efforts to win it back.

The third need in Maslow's hierarchy is *belongingness*, the need to feel accepted by others and as part of a larger social group. Once your survival and security needs have been satisfied, being a "social animal," you seek belongingness and acceptance from other people in your world.

The fourth need in Maslow's hierarchy is *esteem*. You need to feel liked and respected by others so that you can like and respect yourself. This is what triggers your ego or vanity, the need to feel valuable and important.

The fifth need in Maslow's hierarchy is *self-actualization*, the feeling that "you are becoming everything that you are capable of becoming."

Some time later, Maslow postulated two additional, higher-order needs, *truth* and *beauty*. He concluded that once a person had satisfied the five basic needs and felt he was fulfilling his potential, his attention would naturally turn to *truth*, the study of philosophy and religion, and *beauty*, the appreciation of art, music, and beautiful things.

Satisfied Needs Don't Motivate

Maslow's great contribution was his demonstration that each person required the satisfaction of each lower-order need at a certain level before he could progress to the satisfaction of a higher-order need. He also concluded that once a need had been satisfied, it was no longer a motivator of action.

For example, a basic survival need may be food, triggered by the experience of hunger. But once a person has eaten, hunger is no longer a motivator. By the same token, once a person feels secure, the offer of additional security has little motivational power.

The More Basic the Need, the More Powerful the Appeal

Depending upon individual circumstances, people do what they do depending on the level of need most pressing to them at that particular time. In marketing, motivational psychology, and politics, it has been demonstrated that the fastest and easiest way to motivate a person to take action is to appeal to the *lowest* common denominator of needs. This is why most elections are decided by what are called "paycheck issues." People are more motivated to act or to support a candidate if they feel their basic *financial security* is threatened or can be enhanced by supporting that candidate.

In marketing, an appeal to a basic need for a product or service such as, "Would you like to make more money?" is more powerful than saying, "Would you like to improve the quality of your life?" The first question appeals to a basic security need while the second question appeals to a higher-order, self-actualization need. The straightforward appeal to the lower-order need will always trigger a faster, stronger reaction because it is aimed straight at the heart of the E-Factor.

Theory X versus Theory Y

In 1960, Harvard psychologist Douglas McGregor published a groundbreaking book, *The Human Side of Enterprise*, which suggested two visions of people in the workplace, each leading to different forms of motivation in organizations. McGregor called these two views of mankind "Theory X" and "Theory Y."

Theory X was defined as the idea that employees were basically lazy and had to be continually motivated to do their jobs by using the "carrot and stick" method of rewards and punishment. McGregor, on the other hand, postulated Theory Y, which said that people are basically positive, desire to do a good job, and will strive toward excellence in their work if the proper incentives exist.

McGregor divided working conditions into two categories, *hygiene needs* and *motivators*. A hygiene need was defined as including things such as a secure work environment, a decent paycheck, pleasant surroundings, and proper work tools. His conclusion was that the *presence* of these factors did not motivate people to work harder, but if they did *not* exist workers would be demotivated and would not do their best work.

McGregor defined a "motivator" as something more. It was a factor such as special attention from the boss, praise and encouragement, opportunities for promotion and advancement, greater responsibility, and recognition by bosses and coworkers. He concluded that by practicing "Theory Y" management, managers could bring the very best out of their people and achieve the very best and highest quality results.

Theory Z Management

Based on my experience with hundreds of companies, I suggest a third factor, which I call Theory Z. Theory Z says people are neither good nor bad. They are neither positive nor negative. They are neither motivated nor unmotivated. They are merely *expedient*. In everything they do, mentally, emotionally, and physically, they are subject to the overwhelming force of the E-Factor.

According to this assessment, people are *lazy, greedy, ambitious, selfish, vain, ignorant, and impatient,* and they will manifest these qualities in a positive or negative way depending upon the structure of financial and non-financial incentives in the organization. I will explain this in greater detail in Chapter Three.

Taking all of the previous work on motivation into consideration, I have concluded there are seven basic needs that motivate human behavior under all circumstances, for every person.

Seven Levels of Motivation

The first basic motivation is the need for *safety and survival,* just as Maslow identified in his work. If a person's safety and survival is threatened, all other needs are set aside. Safety and survival for oneself and for one's loved ones becomes the predominant focus of all his actions.

As soon as safety and survival are assured, the individual moves up to the second level of need, that of *security.* Again, following Maslow, the need to be secure in one's home, one's job, one's relationship, and to be secure physically, financially, and emotionally, are intense preoccupations of the average person. If these needs are threatened for any reason, the individual becomes preoccupied with them and thinks of nothing else.

In our society, *safety and survival* needs are largely met. Except in extreme situations, people do not give very much thought to whether or not their lives are safe. For this reason, and especially if a person's resources are limited, they are focused much more on achieving satisfactory levels of *security* in all areas. This can mean having a secure place to live, a secure place to work, enough money in the bank to provide against unexpected emergencies, a car that works well, and a feeling that one is secure in his or her world.

As soon as a person feels secure in all of the major areas of his life, his next need immediately becomes *comfort*. He wants to sit down, lie down, dress in comfortable clothes, live in a comfortable home, and generally feel physically comfortable in his world.

Once a person has a certain level of *comfort*, it is no longer a need. Once a person sits down in a comfortable chair, it is very hard to motivate him by offering another chair that is equally as comfortable. Something more is required to get him to take action.

Leisure-Time Activities

The next need that all people have is for *leisure*. Once a person is safe, secure, and comfortable, he or she wants to take it easy, take time off, and relax. People want to take evenings, weekends, and summer vacations off. Leisure-time activities are trillion-dollar industries in affluent societies, in the forms of vacations, travel, cruise lines, visits to Disneyland, national monuments, national parks, and large cities. Leisure-time activities embrace golfing, going to restaurants, flying, sailing, hiking, camping, having friends over for dinner, and socializing.

In advanced societies, where the basic needs of safety, security, and comfort are largely met for the majority of the population, leisure-time activities become the central preoccupation for most people. In any workplace, the main subject of conversation is likely to be what people are going to do after work, on the weekends, and on their vacations. The obsession with watching sporting activities is a fulfillment of the desire for leisure.

Love Makes the World Go Around

As you move up the scale of needs, once leisure needs are satisfied, the individual seeks *love*. Maslow referred to this as an "esteem need," but it is much more than that.

Psychologists say everything we do in life is either to get love or to compensate for lack of love. Most psychological problems in adulthood, and even in childhood, can be traced back to "love withheld."

Children need love like roses need rain. Even adults, with all their excuses, are "love-tropic." We gravitate toward and are most influenced by the people we love and who love us. We never feel whole or complete until we are in a satisfactory love relationship with another person.

It has been said, "Men give love to get sex, and women give sex to get love." There is some truth to this. Recent psychological studies show that when a man is in love with a woman, he is willing to pay substantially more for things that he thinks will please her than he ever would if he were not in a romantic state of mind.

Emotions Distort Valuations

Here's an important point: *emotions distort valuations.* When a person experiences a need intensely, his or her ability to correctly value the cost of satisfying that need often goes out the window. Intense emotion of any kind, love or hate, desire or lust, fear or loathing, can cause a great *disconnect* between the true value of an item and the item itself. Intense emotion causes distorted thinking and irrational behaviors of all kinds.

For example, the manufacturer's list price on a new red sports car may be $30,000. But the cars are sold out and back-ordered for several months. There is only one left. A person who intensely desires that particular car will quite commonly pay a premium of $5,000 to $10,000 to get it, if he can get it *right now*.

A starving person may pay $50 for a hamburger. A person dying of thirst in the desert may pay $100 for a glass of water. A man who is passionately in love with a woman may pay any price to buy her things, and may even steal the money. Emotions distort evaluations, sometimes dramatically. This phenomenon explains many of the otherwise unexplainable behaviors of so many people.

We All Want the Respect of Others

Once a person has satisfied his needs in the areas of *safety, security, comfort, leisure, and love,* the next motivator that arises and drives behavior is the need for respect. As I mentioned before, earning and keeping the respect of others whose opinions we value is a powerful motivator for us. Author William Manchester, writing about his experiences in World War II in the Pacific, noted that people fought and died in terrible conditions rather than running away because they did not want to lose the respect of the men on either side of them.

One element of *vanity* is our idea of how we are thought about and talked about by others. If the people we most respect are men and women of great character and integrity, our desire to live up to their standards will serve as an internal guide to our behaviors, causing us to strive to be the best we can be.

The dark side of the need for the respect of others is often seen in the inner cities, where fatherless boys look up to the Cadillac-driving, money-flashing pimp or drug dealer. They strive to earn his respect by embracing his attitudes and mimicking his behaviors.

The most powerful influence you can have on people who look up to you is to be a *role model* for them. You should strive to talk and behave in such a way that if other people, especially your children and friends, were to behave the same way, they would act and feel better, and their lives would be improved.

Fulfilling Your Potential
The seventh need each person has, once the first six needs have been satisfied to an acceptable level, is the need for *fulfillment.* Each person, deep inside, has an intense desire to fulfill his or her potential as a human being. Some experts say all unhappiness is rooted in a feeling of *frustrated* potential. It is only when you feel that you are enjoying complete self-expression, that you are living the very best life you can live, and achieving the very most of which you are capable, that you feel truly happy.

Maslow found that *self-actualizing* people were the happiest and most fulfilled of all people. Psychologist Carl Rogers referred to this type of individual as the FFP—the *fully functioning person*—and suggested this was the height of personal development to which one could aspire.

Who We Are and What We Want
When we combine these two sides of the coin of human personality, we see that each person is *lazy, greedy, selfish, ambitious, vain, ignorant, and impatient.* At the same time, each person strives throughout their lives to fulfill their needs to get as much s*afety, security, comfort, leisure, love, respect, and fulfillment* as possible, the fastest and easiest way he can.

Money as a Motivator of Behavior
It has been said that, "Money may not be the most important thing, but it's way up there with *oxygen."*
The fastest and easiest way to get the things you want is almost always to have enough *money* to be able to buy them, whatever they cost. For this reason, the desire to quickly and easily acquire as much money as possible is a major motivator of human behavior. But it is not usually money that people really want.

Sometimes I will ask my clients why they want to acquire a lot of money. After thinking about their answer for a couple of minutes, they finally conclude that what they want more than anything else is "freedom." In reality, they see money as a *means* to achieving the freedom they really desire. They define freedom as having enough money so they can get everything they want. They feel that having enough money will enable them to be completely free from worry about *safety, security, comfort, leisure, love, respect, and fulfillment.* They see having lots of money as the fastest way to the good life.

Ten Million Dollars

In our Focal Point Advanced Coaching and Mentoring Program, we do an exercise in *Values Clarification*. When everyone is seated, we hand out individual checks made out to each person in the amount of ten million dollars. Of course, the checks are not cashable, but the idea of receiving ten million dollars gives people an opportunity to fantasize about what they *really* want in their lives.

We then have the participants break into groups, discuss what they would do if they suddenly received ten million dollars, and then report back to the group. We go around the room and write down their answers on a white board or flip chart.

Here is the most amazing discovery: almost everything that our clients would want to do, have, or acquire does not cost any money! When people think of suddenly being financially independent, they immediately think about *quality of life* issues.

As we go around the room, the answers that come back are: *"I would work shorter days and spend more evenings and weekends with my family; I would take a long vacation with my wife; I would join a health club and exercise every day to lose weight and get fit; I would write the book I've always wanted to write; I would get more involved with my church or political party; I would take up painting; I would write poetry; I would reorganize my business and my life; etc."*

This is an exercise you can do as well. Imagine that you received ten million dollars today. What would you do differently in your life if you had all the money you could ever need? You may be surprised at the answers you come up with.

The Lust for Power

This brings me to one of the most important discoveries in all my work on *something for nothing* and the E-Factor. It is the desire for power. This is one of the most destructive forces in the world today, and always has been. If the fastest and easiest way to get all the things you want is to have all the *money* you need, it then follows that the fastest and easiest way to get the money you need is to acquire *power* over people and resources, both in business and at the political level.

The *urge for power*, the need for power, the love of power, the desperate things people will do to get or to hold on to power, explain many of the otherwise unexplainable events taking place in our world today.

Power can be defined as "the ability to control or influence money, people, and resources." It is ultimately the ability to *force* people to do what you want them to do, whether or not it is consistent with their own personal desires.

Power in its *negative* form is used to abuse people and take advantage of situations. Because of the E-Factor, power is initially sought to achieve a result or goal the fastest and easiest way possible. Afterwards, power is sought for its own sake, because of the simple love of power.

The fastest and easiest way to get the *safety, security, comfort, leisure, love, respect, and fulfillment* that a person wants is by acquiring the power, one way or another, that enables him to command those basic needs from others without having to earn them, and with little or no effort on his part. The desire to acquire power is therefore perfectly logical and completely in keeping with the E-Factor and the desire to get *something for nothing.*

Power in Society

Men and women are physically different in many ways. One of the most important differences involves the level of *testosterone* each has from infancy onward. Testosterone is the hormone of masculinity that triggers the drive to dominance, power, and status in society. Men with high testosterone levels are more competitive, aggressive, hostile, bold, assertive, and more determined to move ahead and succeed. The more they satisfy this testosterone-driven impulse, the faster and easier they achieve the *safety, security, comfort, leisure, love, respect, and fulfillment* that they and everyone else want.

In the natural order of things, men do much of what they do to please the women who have the greatest influence over them. In the studies of self-made millionaires, most of whom are men, they found that when a man becomes successful and wealthy, his expenditures on himself stay very much the same as they were when he had less money. But his expenditures on his wife and his family increase dramatically. One of the basic satisfactions of being a successful male is to be a good provider for his wife and children. This is a major motivator for most men.

What Does a Woman Want?

Again, in the nature of things, women like men who achieve high levels of power, status, achievement, and dominance. They like men with high levels of confidence and competence. Biologically, such a male is more capable of providing for her and her offspring. He is more likely to provide a higher standard of living for them and thereby assure that her children will survive and thrive.

Women, because they are more vulnerable than men, especially during pregnancy and the early years of child raising, are much more concerned about satisfying the basic needs of safety and security than men. Solid, hard-working men who get and keep good jobs and provide well for their family are most capable of satisfying these basic female needs. Nature knows what she is doing.

Men's and Women's Brains

The brains of men and women are different. Both men and women have a right brain and a left brain, connected by a mass of tissue called the Corpus Callosum. One of the differences between men's and women's brains is that women use far more of both parts of their brains. They have more connective tissue between the right brain (emotional, intuitive) and the left brain (logical, practical). For this reason, women are generally more stable and balanced in their thinking than men.

Men on the other hand, have smaller bundles of connective tissue between the hemispheres of the brain and are more likely to specialize and even go to extremes, to either left or right brain activities. There are far more *geniuses* in physics, mathematics, medicine, music, and even *cooking* amongst men than amongst women. Most Nobel Prizes are awarded to men, who tend to go to extremes in their areas of genius in the production of Nobel Prize-winning work.

The natural consequence of this brain structure in men is they go to extremes in the achievement of *money* and *power* as well. Virtually all dictators, despots, and totalitarians throughout history have been men.

Money and Power Together

Money starts off as the motivation for an expedient person to fulfill all his needs, for himself and his family. It can soon become an end in itself. Once a person has enough money so that he no longer *worries* about money, it becomes a form of measurement, a scorecard he uses to compare himself against others, as in an athletic competition.

Megalomaniacs and dictators often become obsessed with *power*, to the exclusion of all other considerations. By the same token, many men in business become preoccupied with money, to the exclusion of other things, especially their families. Many in politics begin to live and breathe for political power. Their lives become focused on acquiring, keeping, and using it, almost to the exclusion of anything else. As Henry Kissinger once said, "Power is the ultimate aphrodisiac."

The journalist Ambrose Bierce once defined *fanaticism* as, "Redoubling your efforts after your aim has been forgotten." This often becomes the behavior of people who see their needs either satisfied or threatened depending upon whether they retain or lose their power or money. They become fanatical about it.

Where Do You Rank?

According to James Q. Wilson, the noted sociologist, the first requirement of human society is *hierarchy*. All people throughout the world, in all cultures and nations, need to know the "pecking order" of their society. Who is on top? Who is in the middle? Who is on the bottom? And especially, where do I rank in comparison with this other person?

When two people meet socially, both men and women, the first thing they do is size each other up to determine where the other person ranks in the social and economic hierarchy. Once each is clear regarding the ranking of the other, it is no longer an issue. They can then relax, put it aside, and turn to socializing. Sometimes the relative rank order of importance of a person is obvious. He or she might be better dressed or wear more expensive jewelry. A man may wear an expensive Swiss watch. A woman may wear a designer dress or carry a designer purse. Sometimes hierarchy becomes clear in the way people speak or in the way they are treated by others. In any case, each person continually seeks clues to determine the ranking of the other person in comparison with himself or herself.

How Power Is Acquired

There are different ways that power is acquired in our society. In *business*, power is acquired by getting results, by making decisions that lead to incremental gains in revenues and profits. The most powerful people in the business world are those with the best reputations for achieving *financial* goals in their areas of responsibility.

Some years ago, Antony Jay, in his book *Management and Machiavelli*, explored the role of *playing politics* in corporations as the key to getting more power and influence. He concluded that political gamesmanship might enable a person to get ahead in an organization temporarily. But sooner or later, his ability to perform and get results would catch up with him.

No matter how far ahead he got, or how many times he was promoted, eventually he would be confronted with a demand for *measurable performance.* If the performance was not there, the chair would be kicked out from under the politician, and he would lose his job. He would subsequently have enormous difficulties starting over somewhere else based on his reputation, or non-reputation, for getting results.

In politics however, power is acquired by *winning* votes, separate and apart from any measure of personal accomplishment. Many who go into politics have failed or done poorly in their previous jobs or professions. But in politics, if they have the right connections, personality, support, and issues to win office, they can eventually ascend to positions of power that most of them have never experienced, or even imagined.

The Role of Results

In the private sector the ultimate measure is results. "Did you do the job or not?" This is all that matters. The number one reason that executives, including CEOs of Fortune 500 companies, are demoted or fired is summed up simply as "failure to perform."

In politics however, achieving a result is never necessary. Political activity is not measurable. If you get elected, get along well with your peers and colleagues, keep your head down, and don't make mistakes, you can be successful in politics year after year.

When a person develops the ability to achieve measurable, financial results in business, he enjoys the *safety, security, comfort, leisure, love, respect, and fulfillment* that go with that achievement.

But in politics, it is different. In politics, you are never secure. Because you have not achieved anything measurable to get elected, you are constantly in danger of losing your political office. Any shift in public opinion or scandal, personal or otherwise, can lead to your losing your seat in the next election. One bad call in your political activities can tip the scales, cost you the election, and throw you back into the working force, where you may not have been doing that well before.

The Mother's Milk of Politics

Once a person enters politics, in order to stay in power, he needs more and more money. He must be constantly campaigning and petitioning for campaign donations. This becomes his most pressing need, the one need that enables him to fulfill all his other needs, especially for job security.

Most people who go into politics are *well-meaning*. They have good ideas to help the people who elected them. But once they get into office, they immediately become determined to hold on to their positions. The longer they stay in politics, the less employable they become in the private sector. Often they become desperate to win elections. We'll talk about this later.

The only thing you have to know to understand politics is that everyone is *lazy, greedy, ambitious, selfish, vain, ignorant, and impatient*, including every person who works in or runs a business, or who serves in public office.

Each person strives continually to get more and more *safety, security, comfort, leisure, love, respect, and fulfillment.*

Business versus Politics
In business, the only way you can satisfy these needs in the long term is by producing measurable results, by doing a good job, satisfying customers, building long-term relationships, and keeping the support of the people around you.

In politics however, there is no need to get any other result except to deliver *free money* to the people who voted for you. For example, Congress larded various laws with more than 14,000 "earmarks" (the official word for pork, or free money,) for constituents in 2004 alone. Politicians are *lazy, greedy, ambitious, selfish, vain, ignorant, and impatient* people desperate to hold onto power so that they can continue to satisfy their needs for *safety, security, comfort, leisure, love, respect, and fulfillment* in any way possible. To achieve this, they must deliver.

The Expediency Factor says: *"People strive to get the things they want the fastest and easiest way possible with little concern for the likely consequences of their actions."*

There may be exceptions to the above, but they haven't yet been found. If you want to understand and accurately interpret what is happening in your world, just expect people to act expediently to get the things they want and need the fastest and easiest way possible, and to get *something for nothing* whenever they can.

Now let's look at how people, driven by human nature, by the E-Factor, get the things they want.

> *"Rather fail with honor than succeed with fraud."*
>
> — Sophocles

Chapter Three

Simple as ABC

*"There is only one way to get anybody to do anything,
and that is by making the other person want to do it."*

— Dale Carnegie

What kind of a world is this if everyone is naturally *lazy, greedy, selfish, ambitious, vain, ignorant, and impatient?* How can society survive if everyone is driven by the E-Factor to get more and more of what they want the fastest and easiest way possible with little or no concern for the consequences of their behavior?

At the same time, everyone is motivated by an insatiable desire to achieve *safety, security, comfort, leisure, love, respect, and fulfillment*, manifested by a never ending drive to acquire money and power. What then stops the world from devolving into a war of all against all? The answer to this dilemma comes from understanding how people go about getting the things they want.

The ABC Formula of Human Behavior

Let us divide the way things are done into three parts. We can call the natural instincts that make people *lazy, greedy, ambi-*

45

tious, selfish, vain, ignorant, and impatient, which are summarized in the E-Factor, driving people toward a never ending search for *something for nothing,* as "A."

We can call the natural needs or desires of all people for *safety, security, comfort, leisure, love, respect, and fulfillment,* ultimately manifested in a desire for *power* and *money,* "C." These two elements, "A" and "C," are fixed factors, hard-wired into the human psyche, immutable parts of human nature and human motivation.

The key question, and the only variable in this equation, is: "How does one get from A to C?" We can call this interim step, or *means,* by the letter "B." Together, we can construct the ABC Formula of human activity.

Only Two Basic Ways

There are two ways that you can get anything: you can *earn* it or get it from someone who has earned it, or you can *take* it. There are two ways that you can get someone else to do something: you can *force* him to do it with threats of penalties and punishment, or you can *encourage* him to want to do it, with promises of rewards and benefits.

The only way that you can *stop* many people from engaging in harmful behaviors in the process of getting the things they want, the fastest and easiest way possible, is by making the cost or punishment for expedient behaviors so *high* they are afraid to do it. To stop people from acting expediently, from seeking their own best interests in destructive or criminal ways, you must make the restraints and constraints so costly and severe that people are forced to either curb their natural instincts or suppress them for fear of punishment.

Throughout all of history, dictatorships and tyrannies have been based on forcing people *not* to act expediently or to act contrary to their natural instincts in satisfying their basic needs. This trampling of people and repressing of their natural desires has been the primary use of power throughout history, right up to the present day.

Human beings are, generally speaking, neither bad nor evil; they are merely *expedient*. But when people engage in expedient behaviors which hurt others to get something for little or nothing, and then justify their behaviors, they gradually lose their moral bearings and can become very evil indeed.

A New World Order Begins

In the England of the 1700s, a new way of organizing society appeared based on *voluntary cooperation* rather than compulsion and force. It was called the "market system." The seeds for this open market society had been sown starting as early as 1215 with the signing of the Magna Carta, the first bill to protect the rights and property of the nobles against the unlimited power of the king. Over the next 500 years, the "Divine Right of Kings" was challenged more and more. Parliament and representative government was formed. Laws were written. Rights became codified. Gradually, a system of order based on respect for individual liberty and property took shape.

On this foundation of law and respect for private property, the free market emerged. Today, throughout the world, whenever a legal structure protecting personal and property rights is created, a free market emerges spontaneously. Individuals begin to save, invest, work, take risks, produce products and services for others, and prosperity begins to increase and spread.

The idea of the free market is simple. It is based on *peaceful cooperation* rather than compulsion or coercion. In a free market, each person has the right to enter the market and sell his products or personal services for whatever amount other people are willing to pay. All transactions are voluntary. No one is forced to buy or sell. The only way that expedient people can get the things they want is by offering them to others and making them so attractive that others choose to buy them.

Everyone Benefits

A free market is based on *cooperation* and *voluntary exchange*. The only reason one person trades with another is because he expects to be better off *after* the trade than he was *before* the trade. He values what the other has to sell more than the money that he has, or more than anything else he could acquire for the same amount of money. If a person is not satisfied with the products or services offered, or their prices, he is free to refrain from engaging in any trade or exchange at all.

In 1776, a Scottish philosopher of morals and ethics, Adam Smith, published a book, *The Wealth of Nations*, explaining how this market system worked. This was the first "economics" text book, showing how people who are inherently *lazy, greedy, selfish, ambitious, vain, ignorant, and impatient* can come together in a free market, each motivated by the desires to get *safety, security, comfort, leisure, love, respect, and fulfillment,* and having no choice but to cooperate in such a way that the best interests of each are served.

One of the best known observations from *The Wealth of Nations* is, *"Every individual endeavors to employ his capital so that its produce may be of greatest value...He intends only his own security, only his own gain...By pursuing his own interest he frequently promotes that of society more effectively than when he really intends to promote it."*

The Greatest Miracle

In reality, the free market is the greatest miracle of social cooperation ever conceived of in human society. Because no one can force anyone else to act contrary to their best interests in a free market, everyone must voluntarily cooperate with others if they want to satisfy their own personal needs the fastest and easiest way possible.

In the free market, the best rise to the top. Those who are the most skillful at bringing together and producing products and services that people want and are willing to pay for tend to emerge from the competition and become even more success-ful satisfying customers in more ways. Since every person who controls money or resources wants to earn the highest and best return on those resources, money and resources naturally gravi-tate towards those people with a proven ability to put them to work in the very best way possible. Everyone benefits.

Specialization Becomes Possible

As products and services become more complex, *specialization of labor* develops. Instead of having to produce everything he needs by himself, individuals naturally gravitate toward doing those things for which they have a natural facility, which they can do better, and for which they can earn higher pay and greater rewards.

Competition among individuals and businesses to serve even more customers by giving them more of the things they want faster, better, and cheaper drives *innovation*. Competition for the seven common desires forces people to become even more creative in producing even more and better products and serv-ices for the market. With no intervention, control, or involve-ment by government or any other organized body, the actions of free people in free markets assure the very best and most effi-cient allocation of capital, resources, and labor in the satisfying of customer wants and needs.

The Entrepreneur Takes the Risk

If the entrepreneur guesses wrong and produces a product or service that he cannot sell at a price that yields a sufficient profit to cover the costs of producing it, the losses fall on the shoulders of the entrepreneur and his investors. If the entrepreneur guesses right and brings a product or service to market that customers want in such quantity that he can make a sufficient profit, with which he can invest and produce even more products and services, everyone benefits.

The opportunity to profit in a free market channels the E-Factor into continually seeking better and faster ways to serve consumers. This is why profits are the costs of the future. Where there are profits, there are jobs, opportunities, and hope for the future. Where there are no profits, jobs disappear, companies shut down, and resources move into the hands of people who can use them better.

The Wealth of Nations, which was published in the same year as the Declaration of Independence, became a best seller in the American Colonies in the following years. The ideas of the free market became the bedrock economic principles upon which the American Republic was founded. They still dominate today, even though they are constantly under attack by people and politicians who either do not understand the miracle of voluntary cooperation in open markets or deliberately choose to ignore it in the pursuit of power and money.

Dislike of Freedom and Free Markets

Since people are naturally expedient in that they are *lazy, greedy, selfish, ambitious, vain, ignorant, and impatient*, there are always a substantial number who do not like the idea of being rewarded on the basis of their ability to serve their fellow man in a way that he wants to be served. They detest the idea of the free market. They want rewards without working, rewards that are detached from any merit or any need to satisfy other people. Being human, they want *something for nothing*.

It is the duty and responsibility of politicians and policy makers at all levels to disallow any route to financial success except by *serving* other people in some way. No one should be allowed to benefit except by being voluntarily compensated by those people because they value that service. Allowing people to profit without contributing to the well-being of others is the great dilemma of our day. It threatens the American Dream, which I'll talk about later.

The Structure of Incentives

In the ABC Formula of explaining human behavior, both the "A," who people are, and the "C," what people want, are fixed, immutable factors. The only variable is the "B," how they get from one to the other.

You could call the "B" the "structure of incentives." The structure of incentives determines how a person gets from "A" to "C" the fastest and easiest way possible. Any variation in the structure of incentives will immediately change the behaviors of a certain number of people.

Let us organize the various systems of incentives that are available on a scale of one to ten, from the lowest and least productive system of incentives to the highest.

A system rated at ten would be one where the only way to get anything you want would be to either produce it yourself or cooperate with others to get it with and through them. It would be totally voluntary, based on merit and the perception by each person that he would be better off as a result of working within this system. This is the pure free market system.

At the other end of the scale, a system with a rating of one would be a cultural and economic structure where lying, cheating, deceiving, defrauding, stealing, violence, and murder are the fastest and easiest ways for people to get the things they want.

In criminal societies or organizations, these negative behaviors are the primary ways to acquire *safety, security, comfort, leisure, love, respect, and fulfillment*, especially money and power. Individuals who are the most ruthless and unprincipled in the use of violent means to acquire the things they want inevitably rise to the top, crushing all competition or opposition on the way. You see this in third world tyrannies, drug cartels, and in the aftermath of riots and wars.

Ordering Societies by the Numbers

All groupings of individuals into tribes, societies, and nations can be organized along this scale from one to ten. Peaceful, democratic societies, governed by law, cluster at the top of the scale. Despotic, impoverished societies, ruled by force and tyranny, generally cluster at the bottom. Societies displaying a mixture of the two extremes are arranged along the middle of the scale.

Human nature, however, is like *water*. It flows downhill in and through any crack, crevice, or hole that it can find. Human nature instinctively, impulsively, reflexively drives people to continually strive to get the things they want the fastest and easiest way possible, with little concern for the likely consequences.

As soon as there is any way for people to fulfill their desires *other* than by working and cooperating voluntarily with others, some people find and take advantage of that loophole. And then more and more follow their lead.

Seek the Simplest Explanation

In 1240 AD, the philosopher William of Occam proposed a tool for thinking that became known as "Occam's Razor" because it cut quickly and sharply to the core of any argument or controversy.

What he said was, *"In solving any problem, or explaining any situation, the simplest solution or explanation is probably the correct one."*

Socrates said something similar in Plato's *Dialogues* in 390 BC: *"The correct explanation for any phenomena, or the solution to any problem, is usually the one with the fewest parts or steps."*

The movie *Jerry McGuire*, starring Tom Cruise and Cuba Gooding Jr., became famous for the repeated demand, *"Show me the money!"*

In business or politics there is an old admonition, *"Follow the green!"*

In his book *The Greatest Management Principle*, business author Michael LeBeouf says, *"What gets rewarded gets done."*

The most powerful law in human nature, the foundation of the E-Factor, and the simplest explanation for almost every human behavior is the *Law of Least Resistance*. This law explains why water flows downhill and through any hole or crevice. It also explains why people behave the way they do most of the time.

The simplest explanation, requiring the fewest number of steps to explain any human behavior is the desire of people to get what they want for as little as possible and, if at all possible, for *nothing at all.*

People are what they are: *lazy, greedy, selfish, ambitious, vain, ignorant, impatient,* and constantly striving to fulfill their needs for *safety, security, comfort, leisure, love, respect, and fulfillment* by acquiring money and power. Therefore, the only way to create and maintain peace, harmony, and cooperation is to cut off all avenues to achievement except those of peaceful cooperation and healthy competition aimed at serving and satisfying other people in some way. This is the role of laws and enlightened public policy.

The Development of Personality

Children are completely expedient. They are like little animals, completely uninhibited and unafraid in striving to satisfy their appetites of the moment any way they possibly can, with little or no concern at all for the convenience or comfort of other people.

If you want to raise a healthy, happy child, you have to teach him or her the connection between behavior and consequences, the link between engaging in peaceful, constructive behaviors and getting more of the things he or she really wants.

You must be firm, fair, and not allow him to get what he wants in any other way except by *only* doing those things that are best for him, both in the short term and in the long term.

Children Do What Works

Children will always seek the fastest and easiest way to get what they want. They will seek every way possible to achieve happiness and pleasure and *avoid* discomfort and disapproval. They will engage in positive or negative behaviors, depending on what works and on the structure of incentives set up by their parents.

Children begin to lie and tell half-truths at an early age, not because they are dishonest, but because they are *expedient*. If lying works to get them the "C" that they want and turns out to be the fastest and easiest way for them to satisfy their desires of the moment, they will lie more and more. The more they lie, the more they will rely upon lying as a tool for success, and the better they will become at lying.

Today our society is ensnared in a quagmire of lies pouring out of almost every person and source. Politicians lie repeatedly, brazenly stating things that they know to be false, for short-term political advantage. The news media lie continually, mainly by selectively reporting only those stories and quoting only those people whose statements are consistent with the viewpoint it has already decided to express.

Criminals lie, businesspeople lie, lawyers lie, employees lie, husbands and wives lie. In many areas of daily life, it is automatically assumed that whatever the other person says initially is a lie or a half-truth. This propensity to lie starts in childhood when children find that lying is the fastest and easiest way to get the things they want.

Which Way the Wind Blows

As Alexander Pope wrote, *"As the twig is bent, the tree's inclined."* If a child learns at an early age that he can get what he wants if he does certain things in a particular way, the child will develop in the direction of repeating more and more of that behavior, and will get better and better at it. If it is a good behavior, children will grow up with good character, capable and confident in themselves and their ability to succeed in life.

If children are not carefully and consistently instructed in the importance of being honest and responsible, they will often grow up believing that the way to succeed is by doing as little as possible and deceiving others whenever the opportunity arises.

It is said that *"adults are like children, but with better excuses."* Whenever you meet an adult who has trouble staying "on task" at work or telling the truth, you invariably see the result of a childhood where he was encouraged to behave expediently to get the things he wanted. These habits of thought and action are often difficult to change later in life.

Why the Worst Get on Top

In 1945, at the end of World War II, Frederick Von Hayek, later to be a Nobel Prize-winner in economics, wrote a book entitled *The Road to Serfdom*. In this groundbreaking book, he explained how countries that increasingly relied on government to make and enforce economic and social decisions for the majority put that society on the *road to serfdom*. Perhaps the most important chapter in this book is called, "Why the Worst Get on Top."

In this powerful analysis, Hayek demonstrated that in any system where violent, corrupt, or expedient behavior is rewarded, the most violent, corrupt, or expedient people will eventually rise to the top. They will use their intelligence, cunning, and ability to manipulate such a system to eventually step on, step over, and crush their competition in their lust for the money and power that accrues to the top people.

This insight explained how Hitler, Mussolini, and Tojo rose to the top in Germany, Italy, and Japan. It explained how someone like Stalin, the greatest mass murderer in human history, got to the top of the Soviet system, the most criminal and repressive system known to man. It explains how Mao Tse-tung and the violent men around him were able to take over the Communist movement in China and dominate it for fifty years. This principle explains how Kim Jong Il could dominate North Korea, repressing, starving, torturing, and murdering his own people year after year. It explains a crime boss or the head of a drug cartel.

This principle explains why Saddam Hussein, another mass murderer, could run Iraq year after year with incalculable brutality, based on a sweeping national terror created by the threat of arbitrary arrest, torture, and murder. This principle explains how the worst despots eventually work their way up the food chain to emerge at the top of the heap and the actions they take to keep their money and power once they get there.

Closer to home, this principle explains why violent and cunning men like Jimmy Hoffa, allied with organized crime and continually engaging in bribery, corruption, and theft from union pension funds, could rise to and stay at the top of the Teamsters Union.

Putting the ABC Formula to Work

The only way to build a society based on voluntary cooperation, freedom, liberty, and individual rights is to create a legal structure where people can only enrich themselves by serving others. Only when a free market is created and protected on all sides by legal restraints that block people from getting ahead in any other way but by serving others is it possible to create a peaceful and prosperous society.

It has been said, *"People who do not want to serve others choose rather to rule over them."* There are always people in every society who do not like the idea of having to serve others. They do not like the idea of having their rewards tied to their contribution. They do not like the idea of earning the things they want, satisfying their needs by voluntarily cooperating with others, and depending upon the evaluations of others for their rewards.

The Thievery Gene

Instead, imagine that each person has a "thievery gene" that is part of their mental and emotional DNA. This thievery gene, ready to be activated when any opportunity to get something for little or nothing appears, lurks just below the surface. This natural, knee-jerk, reflexive tendency has to be curbed continually, or it will spring forth in destructive, anti-social behaviors.

If ever there is a way for expedient people to get the results they want faster and easier, especially if it's *something for nothing,* they will find it and take it like water running downhill, finding and flowing through any loophole or crevice that appears. If ever the structure of incentives allows corrupt or anti-social behavior, someone will find a way to take advantage of it. And the worst people will take the most advantage of it and eventually get on top.

The Only True Test of Any Theory

In business and in the free market, the only test for the validity of an idea or course of action is, *"Does it work?"*

The only way that you can tell whether or not a theory or principle is true is by testing it in the real world. *Does it work?* Does it bring about the results desired? Does it bring about better results than another system or theory?

The good news is that in the material world all results are *measurable.* In the business world, all results are measurable in *financial* terms. You can tell if something works in reality by simply looking at the numbers. If it is a good and worthwhile idea, it improves the quality of life and well being of people in measurable terms. If it is not a good idea, it decreases the quality of life and well being of people, again in measurable terms.

Results Speak for Themselves

Throughout the world, whenever freedom and the free market have been introduced, especially into poor nations, they have achieved astonishing results. Asia is one of the best examples. In 1945, both India and Japan were impoverished nations. Most of Japan had been bombed to rubble in World War II. India, extremely poor and underdeveloped, was just emerging from 300 years of British colonization.

Japan introduced the free market. Great monopolies were

broken up, capital poured in, and the free market was encouraged to thrive. Within three decades, Japan became an ultra modern industrial powerhouse, with its people enjoying some of the highest standards of living in the world.

After World War II, India achieved its independence and immediately introduced a socialist system. Private enterprise and the free market were suffocated and replaced by corruption, political cronyism, and controls. As a result, for decades India remained poor, corrupt, and backward, with hundreds of millions of its citizens existing on subsistence wages.

The free market was soon introduced into Hong Kong, Singapore, Taiwan, and Korea. Once it caught on, the economies of these countries boomed. Their living standards rose dramatically. By 1995, the resource-poor island of Singapore surpassed England in annual income per person. Hong Kong became one of the most entrepreneurial and affluent places in the world. Taiwan boomed and flourished, achieving living standards twenty times greater than those of China across the straits.

From 1950 to 2000, the average annual income in Korea went from $200 per year to $10,000 per year, an increase of fifty times! The soaring skyscrapers, beautiful hotels, super highways, and vast industrial complexes of these countries are tributes to freedom, free markets, and free people. These are the kind of results that count.

Thunder Down Under
After World War II, following Britain, New Zealand became an increasingly socialist country. The government interfered with or controlled almost every economic and social activity. Even though New Zealand was resource rich and possessed of a well-educated population, the country stagnated decade after decade. Moving continually in the wrong direction, the govern-

ment placed layer after layer of regulation, controls, and taxes on every part of the New Zealand economy. Unemployment soared. Welfare rolls became unsustainable. Businesses stagnated and young people, seeking opportunities in other lands, moved away year after year.

In the 1980s a labor government under Prime Minister David Lange came to power in New Zealand. For the first time in New Zealand history, the newly elected politicians sat down around the table and looked at each other and agreed, *"This isn't working."* Thus began one of the most profound changes in modern economic history.

Minister of Finance Roger Douglas, seeking ways to turn the New Zealand economy around, set off on a fact-finding tour of the United States and Britain. In the United States, he was introduced to "Reaganomics," the belief that by cutting taxes, slashing regulations, and encouraging the free market, economic activity could be stimulated and prosperity could be created. He went on to England where he learned about "Thatcherism," the idea of getting the government out of most economic activities, curbing the out-of-control power of the labor unions, and encouraging entrepreneurship.

A Man with a Plan
Armed with these ideas, Roger Douglas returned to New Zealand, laid out a new economic plan to install the best ideas of both Reagan and Thatcher, and with the full backing of his government began the transformation of the New Zealand economy.

Within four years the economy had turned around completely. Unemployment had dropped and the welfare rolls were cut in half. The government sold and got out of most companies, corporations, and organizations it controlled. Exports took off, entrepreneurs started new businesses, living standards went up, and prosperity blossomed everywhere.

Four years after Roger Douglas returned from his trip, they had fondly dubbed his policies "Rogernomics," and New Zealand was ranked as the fastest growing industrial country in the world. The free market had worked its magic once again.

Eternal Vigilance Is Necessary

Edmund Burke once wrote, *"The only thing necessary for the triumph of evil is for good men to do nothing."*

The forces of compulsion and coercion, the *something for nothing* people, are always waiting and watching for an opportunity to get back in, no matter how prosperous people become with freedom and free markets. The "thievery gene," activated by the E-Factor and the desire to get *something for nothing*, infects countless people at a deep level, like a cancer that has gone into remission, always capable of being reactivated and spreading throughout the body.

The Killer Emotions

In Chapter One, we discussed the fact that *emotions distort valuations*. There are two negative emotions used to justify and rationalize the worst qualities of human nature: *envy* and *greed*. Like the thievery gene, the emotions of envy and greed lurk just under the surface in the minds and hearts of many people. In combination they generate resentment toward anyone who is more successful in almost any area.

Shakespeare wrote, *"A touch of nature makes the whole world kin."* He said that envy of the successes and accomplishments of others lurks just below the surface in almost every person. It can easily be triggered by an appeal to our sense of *vanity*. People prefer to believe that the reason that someone else is more successful than they are has nothing to do with their own talents, abilities, attitudes, actions, or behaviors. They prefer to believe that people are successful, not because they have worked long and hard to achieve it, but because they have simply been "lucky."

Democratic congressman Richard Gephardt said a couple of years ago, *"Those who have been successful at the gaming tables of life must be forced to share their winnings with those who have not done as well."* In his view, material success, usually attained after many years of hard work, was the equivalent of casino gambling. This is the kind of thinking that dominates much of the policy making in Washington and in the individual states.

Someone Else Is Always to Blame

Each person has a deep need to rationalize away his own perceived failures and deficiencies. The easiest way to do this is to blame *someone else* for your problems. Politicians, eager to get votes by appealing to the lowest common denominator of human nature, will eagerly step forward to encourage people to believe that the reason that they are not doing well is because others are doing better.

Of course, this is the same as saying, "The reason you are sick is because someone else is healthy." The reason you are doing poorly is because someone else is doing well. The reason you are unfit or overweight is because others are fit and trim. The argument is absurd, but reason and rationality have no place when it comes to emotions such as envy and greed, especially when they are combined with resentment.

The Worst Negative Emotion

Envy is perhaps the worst of the negative emotions. Envy hurts and often destroys the possessor of the emotion, but it has no offsetting benefits or pleasures. If you engage in the cardinal sins of gluttony or lust, at least you get some pleasure or satisfaction in the short term. But with envy, you only feel angry, hostile, resentful, and often depressed and worthless. There is no payoff, and it doesn't even hurt or affect the person or persons it is aimed at. It only hurts the possessor.

The emotions of envy and greed, combined with resentment, always require there be an "enemy." Someone must be to *blame*. If someone is to blame, someone must be punished. That person must be taxed, regulated, or even prosecuted. The more the envious person thinks about how evil this blameworthy person is, the angrier he becomes and the more justified he feels in demanding this person be made to suffer in some way.

Punish the Rich

In a free society, where people are paid based on their willingness and ability to serve others, the enemy is always "the rich." These people are loosely defined as anyone who is doing better than the average. Almost all economic and social policy in America and throughout Europe is based on envy and resentment of the successful and is motivated by a desire to punish them in some way.

A healthy, normal person sees himself as *responsible* for his own life. He does not blame his problems or his life situation on anyone but himself. He never complains or criticizes others who are more successful, or condemns people for doing well. If he is not happy with his situation, he gets busy and takes action to improve it. He doesn't blame other people for his own personal problems.

The Perception of Victimhood

Weak people, on the other hand, people who lack the character that only comes from serious thinking and the practice of self-mastery and self-discipline, are easily convinced that *others* cause their problems and deficiencies. This frees them from any responsibility to do anything for themselves. Envy, resentment, and blaming others turn the possessor of these emotions into a *victim*.

The perception of victimhood makes him feel weak and inadequate, helpless and hopeless. It makes him simultaneously angry, discouraged, and capable of being easily manipulated into supporting any politician or activist who promises to punish with taxes and regulations the imagined cause of his own personal problems. This always turns out to be "the rich." No one ever envies a failure or lobbies to punish them with taxes and regulations.

Instead of doing something to improve his situation, the victim, driven by the E-Factor, motivated by the desire to get *something for nothing,* supports anyone who promises to get him *free money* with no effort on his part.

Your Mental Immune System

Almost anyone can catch a cold if he allows himself to become overtired and susceptible to it. In the same way, almost anyone can catch the *something for nothing* virus if he is not continually on guard. We are all susceptible. Once SFN strikes, it can quickly corrupt all your mental and emotional programs.

We are surrounded by people who will tell us repeatedly that we are entitled to free money at the expense of others. Even though this is impossible in the *long* run, it is a fantasy that too many people want to believe.

To immunize yourself against the temptations of the negative emotions of envy, resentment, greed, and the desire to get *something for nothing,* I have prepared a pledge for each person to read and sign. Here it is:

The Responsibility Pledge

I accept complete responsibility for myself, my life, my family, my financial situation, and everything that happens to me.

I am a completely free, proud, self-reliant individual. I look to myself for the answers to my questions and the solutions to my problems.

I am a complete optimist. I look for the good in every situation. I seek the valuable lesson in every setback or obstacle. I think about my goals and how I can achieve them most of the time. I focus on the solution rather than the problem.

I am not a victim. I refuse to complain, condemn, or criticize. If I am not happy with a situation, I take action to change it. I blame no one for any aspect of my life.

I recognize that there is a fair and full price that must be paid for anything worthwhile. I do not try to get something for nothing. I refuse to accept something for nothing, and I do not support any person, process, or policy that attempts to give me or anyone else anything to which I or they are not justly entitled to as the result of personal hard work and sacrifice.

I am a successful, happy person. I am grateful for my life and my opportunities. I believe that everything in the universe is conspiring to make me happier, healthier, and more prosperous.

I have an attitude of gratitude toward everyone and everything.

_____

Signed

How do you feel as you read over this pledge? Are you hesitant or eager to sign your name at the bottom? How you think and feel when you read this pledge to yourself will tell you a lot about your philosophy of life. How others react and respond when you show this pledge to them will tell you a lot about how they think and feel, as well.

In the next chapter, you will learn how you can get the E-Factor and the universal desire to get *something for nothing* under control.

"Good thoughts bear good fruit; bad thoughts bear bad fruit."

— James Allen

Chapter Four

Character Reigns Supreme

"Honesty is the first chapter of the book of wisdom."
— Thomas Jefferson

The fundamental glue that holds our society together is the quality of *character*. It is the foundation of happy families, companies, and organizations. It assures survival, civility, and the blessings of peaceful cooperation. Your character is the crystallization of your true values and beliefs, your innermost convictions. It is the summary of the qualities and virtues by which you live. As Ralph Waldo Emerson said with regard to character, *"What you are shouts at me so loudly that I can't hear a word you say."*

The aim of virtually all religions is to establish and encourage people to develop higher levels of character. A major focus of philosophy throughout the ages has been to identify the qualities of character most conducive to success in personal and public life. Dr. David McClelland of Harvard, in his book *The Achieving Society,* wrote that *"the direction of a society is largely determined by the qualities of character that are most admired in that society."*

As Shakespeare wrote, *"He who steals my purse steals trash; but he who steals my good name, steals all."* Character is everything.

Choices and Decisions

Everything you do in life involves a *choice*, a decision on your part. Because you have so many options, you are constantly choosing among alternatives, between what you value *more* and what you value *less*. You can only do one thing, or choose one thing at a time. When you are under pressure and forced to choose, you reveal your true self, your real values, and your genuine inner convictions. When you choose, you tell yourself and others what is most important to you.

Your *actions* always tell you and others what you truly value the most, at that moment. It is not what you say, or wish, or hope, or intend that reveals your character. It is only what you *do* at the moment of choosing, especially when you have to choose between what is right and what is expedient.

The only way people can be held back from acting expediently in ways harmful to themselves and others is by means of *internal* or *external* constraints. An internal constraint exists when you decide by and for yourself to do what is right, no matter what the temptation. An external constraint is something imposed upon you by law and society or by circumstances that forces you to do the right thing or behave in a certain way, whether you want to or not.

The Hierarchy of Character

The best restraint you can put on the E-Factor in yourself is internal, chosen by yourself, rather than external, imposed upon you by someone or something else. As Herodotus wrote, *"Only when a man's battle begins with himself is he really worth anything."*

There is a hierarchy of *social class* in every country. In every society, some people are more highly developed and more worthy of respect and esteem than others. Where we rank in comparison with others is an essential part of our self-image and self-respect. We all need to know the relative hierarchical *order* of people around us. We need to know who is above us and who is below us socially and economically.

The primary hierarchy in advanced societies is that of *character.* The greater the qualities of character one has, the better a person he is, and the more esteemed and respected he is by most of the people around him. Character development is therefore a lifelong process and never-ending goal.

The Core Quality of Character

The core quality of character is *integrity.* This can be measured by how absolutely honest one is with himself and others. The depth of your integrity largely determines the strength of your commitment to each of your other values.

Character can therefore be best defined and measured *as the degree to which a person adheres to higher values.*

A person of great character is one who would never compromise his or her "sacred honor" under any circumstances. In other words, a person with character would never act *expediently* in such a way that it would harm others, no matter what the temptation. He would always do the right thing in any situation.

The Measurement of Character

Strength of character can be measured on a scale from one to ten, from lowest to highest. In addition, each separate quality or virtue can be organized on a scale of intensity from one to ten.

Everyone possesses almost every virtue or quality to some degree. Even the most dishonest and disreputable person will demonstrate a certain amount of integrity in dealing with certain other people. That's why it is said that there is "honor among thieves."

How high a person ranks on the scale of one to ten in any particular virtue and in the measure of character overall is determined by the percentage of the time that individual practices that quality throughout his or her daily life.

Some people have high, unshakeable levels of character which they would never compromise. They would rather suffer or even die than break their word or go against their deepest values.

Others have varying degrees of character, depending upon the circumstances and the temptations of the moment. They have the modern curse of "situational ethics." They are expedient when it comes to character.

At the bottom of the scale, there are those who have no character at all. There are no principles or values that they would not compromise if the expected reward was attractive enough. These are the kind of people who become habitual criminals. When people with no character, no internal constraints, get into positions of power or authority, their effect on others can be devastating.

Weakness of Character

The E-Factor drives everyone to be *lazy, greedy, ambitious, selfish, vain, ignorant, and impatient,* but to people lower down on the character scale, expedient behavior is almost irresistible. Because of their backgrounds, because they are weak in character, they cannot stop themselves from impulsively and reflexively acting expediently. They cannot resist the striving to get *something for nothing*, at the slightest temptation or the first opportunity.

You see this character weakness most commonly in criminal behavior. Habitual criminals cannot *not* steal. They have convinced themselves over time that the very best, fastest, and easiest way to get the things they want is to take them from others. They don't consider any other options.

You see this weakness of character in people who have *addictions* to food, drugs, alcohol, and tobacco. They are not strong enough to stop themselves from indulging in the immediate sensory pleasures of these substances. No one starts off with an addiction. But by giving in to the E-Factor over and over, they finally reach the point where they are incapable of stopping themselves from ingesting substances that are harmful to them.

Worst of all, you see this weakness of character amongst people who are too weak to resist the blandishments of various forms of welfare, entitlements, and free money from the government or any other source. They cannot stop themselves. And no amount is ever enough.

The Law of Incremental Commitment

One of the most important principles in understanding human behavior is the *Law of Incremental Commitment.* This law says that people do not leap from self-sufficiency and independence into the trap of welfare and dependence on government in one step. They do not go from being law-abiding members of society to habitual criminals in one act. This evolution takes place gradually over time.

Like an alcoholic who starts with one drink after work in the evening, the individual who becomes addicted to free money from the government starts by taking a single payment when he is particularly vulnerable or broke. Just as one drink leads to another for an alcoholic, one welfare payment or handout leads to the next for a person who gradually becomes dependent on government. Soon he becomes addicted and unable to resist the next handout.

It is the same with criminals. They start off stealing small amounts and then larger and larger amounts, especially if they get away with it at the beginning. I'll dedicate a whole chapter to this later.

Justification and Rationalization

Most people know there is something inherently wrong with taking *free money*, with living off the government, with being dependent and making no contribution to the society in which they live. To compensate for this deep inner feeling of unease, people who are getting *something for nothing* create elaborate justifications and rationales to explain to themselves, and to others, why they are entitled to this free money.

Every rationale or excuse comes back to the same explanation. They see themselves as victims who are entitled to free money as compensation for something society has done to them or not done for them. Simultaneously, they see the people who supply free money as being "guilty" for some reason, and therefore justly required to provide the free money to the victim.

Welfare workers are often surprised when welfare recipients tell them that not only are they *entitled* to welfare payments, but people who do not take welfare are "suckers." Many welfare recipients have actually convinced themselves they are superior to people who work for a living and pay the taxes off of which they live.

The Master Quality of Success

The foundation quality of character is *self-discipline*. Self-discipline is manifested in several ways: self-control, self-mastery, and self-restraint. Elbert Hubbard once wrote, "Self-discipline is the ability to make yourself do what you should do, when you should do it, whether you feel like it or not." This is a good definition to work from.

On a scale of one to ten, men and women of admirable character have high degrees of self-discipline. Men and women with weaker characters have little or no discipline at all. They are basically out of control. They cannot constrain or restrain themselves.

Every minute, every hour, and every day, the battle rages back and forth between the forces of the *E-Factor* and the power of *self-discipline*. The mental and emotional contest goes on between doing what is fun, easy, and expedient, on the one hand, and doing what is hard, necessary, and right, on the other hand. Whichever of these two contesting influences wins in the heart and mind of the individual determines the happiness, success, and status of that person both in the moment and throughout his life.

The Common Denominator of Success
Some years ago a businessman, Herbert Grey, engaged in an eleven-year quest to see if he could discover the *"common denominator of success."* Eventually, he found it.

He concluded that the major difference between successful people and failures was that *successful people make a habit of doing what unsuccessful people don't like to do.*

And what are these things that failures don't like to do? It turned out they were the *same* things successful people didn't like to do either. But successful people disciplined themselves to do them anyway—getting up earlier, working harder, and staying later—because successful people realized that these were the prices one had to pay to rise above the average.

As a wise man once said, *"There are always two choices, two paths to take. One is easy. And its only reward is that it's easy."*

The "S" Word Precedes All Success

Perhaps the most important word in success and achievement is sacrifice. Successful, happy people are willing to make the necessary sacrifices each day, and throughout their lives, to enjoy greater rewards and benefits at a later time. They are willing to pay the price of success over and over again until they attain it.

Motivational speaker Dennis Waitley says, *"The difference between successes and failures is that unsuccessful people prefer activities that are tension-relieving while successful people prefer activities that are goal-achieving."* Successful people are willing to pay the price in terms of self-discipline, self-mastery, and self-control, in advance, in order to enjoy the future rewards of success.

Taking It Easy

This temptation to do what is fun and easy, rather than what is hard and necessary, is obvious everywhere. It is normal and natural and driven by the twin desires for *comfort and leisure.* Once a person has safety and security, he immediately turns to thoughts of comfort and leisure, sometimes to the exclusion of almost everything else.

Most people prefer to chat with coworkers, go out for drinks after work, eat, watch television, socialize with friends, and generally engage in "tension-relieving" activities rather than do more productive and helpful things in terms of their future lives, families, and careers.

According to several studies, the average American today, although paid for a forty-hour workweek, works only about thirty-two hours. According to Robert Half International, fully 50 percent of this time is wasted, spent on idle conversations with co-workers, personal business, phone calls, and extended coffee breaks and lunches. Of the approximately sixteen hours a person actually works, much of that is spent working inefficiently or on low-value activities.

Developing the Habits of Success

Fully 95 percent of your success will be determined by your habits. As Ed Foreman said, *"Good habits are hard to form, but easy to live with; bad habits are easy to form but hard to live with."*

Whatever you do *repeatedly* over and over soon becomes a new habit. If you get into the habit of chatting and socializing at work, very soon your interactions and conversations with your coworkers will begin to take up your whole day. Meanwhile, the things you have been hired to accomplish, the key result areas of your job, will be neglected. Over time, you will be passed over for promotions and raises. Your career will slip into a backwater, and others will move ahead of you.

If you are not careful, instead of accepting responsibility for yourself and your situation, you will begin to blame others—your boss, colleagues, coworkers, and customers—for your situation. Occasionally, people who cannot discipline themselves to do their jobs properly not only get laid off or fired, but sometimes become violent and shoot up their work places.

Self-Discipline Is Like a Muscle

The good news is that self-discipline is like a muscle. Every exercise of self-discipline, in any area, strengthens all your other disciplines. In Dorothea Brande's book *Wake Up and Live*, she spends an entire chapter explaining how to develop your "discipline muscles." From getting up in the morning and making your bed immediately, through to planning and preparing each day, being punctual, keeping your word, completing your assignments on time, and following through on your commitments to yourself and others. She explains how you can train yourself to become a highly disciplined person. *"Success is tons of discipline."*

The bad news is that every *weakness* in discipline, in any area, weakens all your other disciplines as well. They are not separable. The best part of the practice of self-discipline is that each time you discipline yourself to do something you know you should do, your self-esteem goes up. You like yourself more. Your *self-image* improves. You respect yourself more and are more respected by others. Every act of self-discipline makes you a more confident, happier person. When you practice self-discipline regularly, in small and large matters, you feel good about yourself.

On the other hand, when you give in to the E-Factor, when you do the fastest and easiest thing and choose what is fun and easy over what is hard and necessary, your self-esteem goes *down*. You feel angry and frustrated. Your self-image worsens, and your self-respect declines. You become a weak and irresolute person.

The Time of Your Life

In 1964, Dr. Edward Banfield published *The Unheavenly City*, describing his twenty-five years of research into success in America and other countries. He updated it in 1989, concluding nothing had changed in the ensuing quarter century. The focus of his inquiries was to seek out the real reason for upward socioeconomic mobility in American society. He asked: *"Why is it that some people move up socially and economically in the course of their lifetimes, and others do not?"*

He carefully compared factors such as family background, intelligence, schools or colleges attended, industry or business worked in, marriage and divorce, different cities or regions of the country, and personal talents and abilities. What he found was that these factors were *necessary but not sufficient.* Each of these factors was helpful, but they were not enough. There did not seem to be any direct correlation between any of these factors and upward social mobility. Many people who started with every advantage failed to accomplish much, and many actually regressed socially and economically over the course of their lifetimes.

Some people went to top universities and then went on to live mediocre lives. Others dropped out of high school and went on to head up major industries. Some people had high IQs and ended up going nowhere. Others with average IQs became extremely successful, respected people within their communities. Some successful people grew up with every blessing of family background, while others who became successful had immigrated to the U.S. knowing no one and not even speaking the language.

Long-Term Thinking

After several years of research, he finally stumbled on the real reason for socio-economic advancement and upward mobility. He called it *long-time perspective.* He defined time perspective as *the amount of time that a person takes into consideration when deciding what he is going to do in the present.*

He found that successful people tend to be future-oriented. They think about the future much of the time. They project five, ten, and even twenty years into the future in considering their current decisions. Especially, they carefully calibrate what would

be likely to happen in the future if they were to take a certain action in the present. As a result of thinking this way, they made better and better decisions in the short term that led to better and better results in the long term.

Consider the Secondary Consequences

Henry Hazlitt, in his book *Economics in One Lesson*, explained that the ability to accurately predict the *secondary consequences* of your actions is the true mark of the superior intellect.

The initial reason for every action is *expedient*. It is focused on the *primary consequences* of the act, which are always positive, or the individual would not act in the first place. It is driven by the desire to get the things you want faster and easier than any other way available to you, with little concern for what is likely to happen as a result.

But *superior* thinkers are more concerned about the long-term consequences of their actions. They play down the chessboard of life. They think several moves ahead. They analyze and evaluate what is likely to happen if they were to do or not do something. Only then do they decide to act.

The Superior Thinker

Both Hazlitt and Banfield came to the same conclusion. Long-term thinking dramatically improves short-term decision-making. The more you develop the habit of thinking long term, the better decisions you make in the short term. The better decisions you make in the short term, the more likely it is you will create the long-term future you desire.

It is the man or woman who thinks long term, who does things in the present that can have positive results or benefits in the future, who is the one most likely to succeed, and who is going to be the happiest and most fulfilled along the way.

As I said earlier, one of the most important words in life and long-term success is *sacrifice*. The ability to delay gratification, to practice self-denial and self-restraint in the short term, leads to greater success and rewards in the long term. There is a saying, *"Short-term pain leads to long- term gain, but short-term gain often leads to long-term pain."*

In our society, we esteem long-term thinking and acting above almost any other quality. Surveys to determine the most respected Americans always come to the same conclusions. Doctors, judges, and professionals, people who have invested many years in study, preparation, and experience to get where they are, always rank as the most respected people in our society. We recognize they have made extraordinary investments of time and huge sacrifices over many years to reach their present positions.

The Low Road to Failure

The opposite of long-term thinking is the habit of focusing on *immediate gratification* in the short term. This focus blinds people to the possible long-term consequences of their actions. Short-term thinking causes people to give into the E-Factor and lies at the root of most of our personal, political, and social problems today.

For example, a young man goes to school, fools around, is inattentive to his studies, gets poor grades, and finally drops out to get a job and buy a car. In the short term, he has a car and money, but at the price of a lifetime of low wages and limited possibilities.

Another common example of short-term thinking is when labor unions strike for higher-than-market wages (airlines, steel, automobile manufacturing) at the long-term price of making their companies and industries non-competitive with non-union or foreign suppliers. They get increased wages in the short term at the price of permanently crippling their companies and industries in the long term, throwing them out of work permanently.

For example, the higher union wage premium in the railroad industry accounted for 64 percent of the decline in union jobs over the last twenty years. From 1973 to 1987 alone, employment on railroads dropped from 520,000 to 249,000. These jobs are gone forever. Short-term gain led to long-term pain.

Another example of short-term thinking that is damaging our country is when the government continually increases expenditures, expands programs, adds entitlements, boosts budgets, and hires more staff at inflated salaries at the long-term cost of huge government deficits that will have to be repaid by our children and grandchildren.

Many people quit their jobs in the short term to live off unemployment at the long-term price of diminished self-respect and lower lifetime earnings.

Criminals engage in robberies, burglaries, and theft to get immediate money at the price of long prison sentences and ruined lives in society.

People in the workplace only do what they have to do to earn a paycheck and then spend their time socializing and watching television, at the long-term price of underachievement and failure in life.

Over all, men and women continually do what is fun and easy in the short term, rather than what is hard and necessary, at the long-term price of never fulfilling their unique potentials as human beings.

The Education of the Young

Aristotle wrote, *"All advancement in civilization begins with the development of character in the young."*

The greatest need for a child is to learn the core values of *self-*

discipline, honesty, integrity, responsibility, courage, compassion, hard work, generosity, and persistence. A child learns these virtues by being instructed by his parents and by seeing his parents demonstrate them in their daily lives.

Once a child has been taught these values and virtues, he must then be encouraged to develop the self-control and personal mastery necessary to live by them, no matter what the temptation of the moment.

The Key to Life-Long Success

The most important quality for a child to learn is *self-discipline*, the ability to *delay gratification*. This quality will have an impact on the child for the rest of his life. In an experiment at Harvard some years ago, they tested this idea. They seated several children under the age of five around a table and gave each of them a candy. They told these children that, if they could refrain from eating this candy, they would receive two candies when the experimenter came back into the room.

They then watched the children through a one-way mirror. Some of the children gobbled up the candy immediately. Others did not. As the time passed, the children who were holding themselves back from eating the candy engaged in all kinds of behaviors to control themselves. Some closed their eyes. Some covered up the candy. Some looked away from the candy. Others sang or spoke to themselves. Most of them finally gave in and ate the candy.

Twenty years later, they followed up on these children. What they found was quite revealing. There turned out to be a direct relationship between how quickly the child ate the candy after the researcher had left the room and how successful and happy he had turned out to be in adult life. The ones who had gobbled the candy immediately were dissatisfied, struggling, and working at lower-level jobs. The ones who held themselves back from eating the candy were more successful, happier, and better paid. This is why successful author Napoleon Hill once wrote, *"Self-discipline is the master key to riches."*

The Need to Lead

The greatest need we have today, in every area, is for men and women to practice the values of *integrity, discipline, responsibility, courage, and long-time perspective*, both as individuals in the workplace and with their families. These are the key qualities of leadership.

Our society needs leaders at all levels who practice the principles that lead to long-term success. Especially, we need people in positions of authority and political power to support and encourage others, whose lives and work they influence, to develop character and resist the tendency to act expediently in ways harmful to themselves and others.

Everyone needs to take "The Values Pledge" (at the end of this chapter), live by it, and then encourage others to live by it. It is only the solid bulwark work of character, based on values, virtues, long-term thinking, and the accurate assessment of secondary consequences, that can curb and mitigate the destructive influences and behavior of the E-Factor.

Live In Truth

The philosopher Immanuel Kant postulated what he called "The Universal Maxim." He suggested *"you should live your life as though your every act were to become universal law for all other people."* I wrote earlier that the very best judge of truth for you is to ask, "Is this true for me?" If everyone was encouraged to live as though their every act were to become a universal principle for all others, most government policies and programs would be abolished overnight. The fact is, the only way many *something for nothing* programs and policies in government and society can be put forward is with the hope that most people will *not* take advantage of them.

Think about it. What if everyone went on welfare? What if everyone got unemployment insurance? What if everyone applied for every government program available to them? What if everyone dedicated themselves to doing the very least amount of work they could get away with? What if everyone began spending all their time trying to get free money from anywhere that it might be available? The answer is that our society would collapse overnight.

Four Questions to Stay on Track

There are *four* questions you can ask and answer every day to keep yourself on track in each part of your life. First, ask yourself, *"What kind of a world would this world be if everyone in it were just like me?"*

When you ask and answer this question honestly, you will admit that if everyone in the world was just like you, this would probably not be the best of all possible worlds. Look into yourself and think about some of the things you could change or do differently to become a better "citizen of the world."

The second question you can ask is, *"What kind of a country would America be if everyone in it were just like me?"*

This is one of the most important questions we can ask and answer of ourselves. If everyone in America did the same things you did, every single day, would America be a better, happier, healthier, and more prosperous democracy? If not, what are some of the changes you could make in your behaviors that would make America a better place?

The third question you can ask is, *"What kind of a company would my company be if everyone in it were just like me?"*

If you are honest with yourself, you will see different things you could do to become a more valuable and important *contributor* to your company. Perhaps you could start a little earlier, work a little harder, or stay a little later. Perhaps you could volunteer for more assignments or upgrade your knowledge and skills as they relate to your job. How could you become the very best person you could possibly become at your work?

The final question, and perhaps the most important, is, *"What kind of a family would my family be if everyone in it were just like me?"*

If everyone in your family behaved the way you do and treated everyone else the way you treat them, would your family be a warmer, happier, and more loving group of people? What could you do, starting today, to be a better family member?

Take the High Road

The true mark of the superior person is that he sets high standards for himself and refuses to compromise those standards for any reason. He sees himself as a role model for others. He behaves at all times as if everyone were watching, even when no one is watching.

The truly superior person does not give in to the forces of expediency. He does not seek something for nothing. He refuses to take anything to which he is not entitled. He insists upon earning everything he gets. He practices the Golden Rule and treats everyone the way he would like to be treated. He sets high standards for himself and continually strives to meet those standards. If everyone in America were to take the pledge on the following page, this would be a better country in every way.

The Values Pledge

"I hereby resolve to live by the values of integrity, honesty, truth, and courage, to remain true to the highest standards I know, and to be the best person I can possibly be.

I will not compromise what I know to be right for any reason. I will live my life as though my every act was to become a universal law for everyone else."

_____

Signature

Let us look now at the current dilemma we find ourselves in today, the problems and difficulties that the out-of-control force of the E-Factor, multiplied by the desire to get something for nothing, has gotten us into, and how we can get out of them.

> *It is the eternal struggle between these two principles—right and wrong....They are the two principles that have stood face to face from the beginning of time and will ever continue to struggle....It is the same spirit that says, "You work and toil and earn bread, and I'll eat it."*
>
> — Abraham Lincoln

Chapter Five

The Current Dilemma

"All of life is action and passion, and not to be involved in the actions and passions of your time is to run the risk of not having truly lived."

— Plotinus

In Lewis Carroll's book, *Alice In Wonderland*, Alice is arguing with the Mad Hatter over a ridiculous idea he has suggested. Alice says, *"You can't believe something like that; it's impossible."*

The Mad Hatter replies, with some pride, *"Nonsense! I've developed the ability to believe at least two completely impossible things every morning before breakfast."*

Likewise, the United States and much of the world is filled with people who proclaim and declare completely impossible things, usually out of a combination of both ignorance and expediency.

Saying Something Doesn't Make It True

Clamoring voices, detached from reason and oblivious to both human and personal experience, have resorted to what is called *argumentation by assertion*. They feel that if they can say or write an impossible thing often enough, in enough different ways, it will somehow begin to come true, like a fairy tale.

In propaganda, as developed to an art by the Nazis in the 1930s, this is known as "the big lie" method of influencing public opinion. This theory says that if you repeat a big lie often enough, eventually people will come to believe it, even if it contains no truth at all.

Once people start to believe something, even if it is completely false, they develop a form of *selective perception*. They begin to seek and find more and more evidence to support their new belief.

Once a person has started to believe something, he selectively ignores and excludes any and all information or evidence that contradicts the new chosen belief. He becomes more and more convinced of the accuracy and rightness of the idea. Finally, he becomes impervious to any evidence to the contrary and even attacks those who disagree.

All Beliefs Are Learned

It is important to remember that no one is born with any religious, political, social, or personal beliefs. All are learned as the result of instruction, experience, and repetition.

What is worse, many beliefs that people hold dearly are *false*. They are not only not backed up by fact but flatly contradicted by all available evidence. *Assertion is not proof.* Only facts are proof.

Abraham Lincoln was once arguing a point with his cabinet minister, William Stanton. He stopped the conversation and asked, *"If you call a dog's tail a leg, how many legs would the dog now have?"*

Stanton quickly replied, *"Five."*

"No," replied Lincoln. *"Calling a dog's tail a leg doesn't make it a leg."*

Here is the point. Believing something, wanting something to be true, has no bearing whatever on whether it is true or not. Repeating a false claim or fact does not make it true.

Napoleon Hill, who studied the most successful and richest men in America for twenty-five years, concluded that the best advice he could give others was, *"Never try to violate natural laws and win."*

The Great Law

Aristotle first propounded the Iron Law of the Universe, the foundation principle of Western civilization, in about 350 BC at his Academy outside of Athens. This law was subsequently known for 2000 years as "The Aristotelian Principal of Causality." He said simply, *"We live in an orderly universe governed by law. Therefore, everything that occurs happens for a reason, whether or not we know what that reason is."*

Up to that time, most people believed that the world was controlled by the gods on Mount Olympus or by random chance. After Aristotle propounded his dictum, people began to realize there is an explanation for every event.

Today, we call this the *Law of Cause and Effect*. It says for every effect, there is a specific cause or series of causes. Nothing happens by accident. If you want to get or duplicate a particular effect, you must first identify and then duplicate the cause of that effect.

This is the foundation principle of all of modern science and technology. When someone refers to a "scientific formula," he is saying that this formula has a proven cause and effect relationship. As a result, it has a high degree of "replicability." Something is scientifically validated only if it can be replicated by someone else implementing the same cause-effect relationships as the original scientist.

Throughout history, man has never "invented" any law or principle in any area— science, mathematics, physics, economics, or medicine. He has only "discovered" them. All *laws*, such as gravity, have always existed. All principles, such as those used in mathematics, have been true for all time.

Some Things Never Change

Some things are always true. They never change. This is especially true with regard to human nature, the expediency factor, the desire for *something for nothing*, the lust for money and power, and the principles of economics that predict and explain wealth and affluence, or poverty and deprivation.

Here is the basic law. *Nothing comes from nothing.* In our material world, something must be produced before it can be consumed. Everything comes from something.

This means if someone consumes without producing, someone else must produce without consuming.

All wealth is created, produced by one or more people. There is no "causeless" or "unearned" wealth or production. To give any economic good or money to anyone, you must first take it away from someone else.

You Can Only Get Out What You Put In

In the New Testament, we first learn of the Law of Sowing and Reaping. It says, *"Whatsoever a man soweth, that also shall he reap."*

This law says you cannot reap without sowing *first*. It also says you cannot sow one thing and reap another. You cannot sow wheat and reap barley. You cannot sow apples and get pears. Whatever you put in, you get out. This is a universal, immutable law.

Notice the order of this law. It says, "First you sow, and then you *reap*." It is not vice-versa, as many would like to believe.

Sir Isaac Newton, one of the most important figures in scientific history, explained the Law of Action and Reaction. He said, *"For every action, there is an equal and opposite reaction."* In other words, whatever you do, you cause something to happen in equal measure. What you put in, you get out. You cannot do something without triggering a consequence of some kind.

For all of human history, no one argued against these laws. They were accepted as "facts of life." Each person saw that his role in life was to somehow organize his activities in harmony with these laws in order to survive and thrive.

The Story of Civilization

For much of human history, people knew that you had to first produce something before you could consume it. The development of civilization has involved people's coming together in villages and towns, then cities and nations, to work cooperatively in order to be more productive. Individuals joined communities from the very beginning because, being expedient, they felt that the fastest and easiest way to get the things they wanted was to work together with others to produce more for everyone.

Most of the wars of history have been aimed at loot and plunder, taking lands that others had cleared and cultivated and assets others had manufactured and created. Governments of countries, kingdoms, nations, and empires developed to protect the populace from the predatory actions of aggressors who might try to invade and rob the citizens of the goods and crops they had produced.

For hundreds of years, progress was slow and halting. After the growth and expansion of the Roman Empire, civilization and prosperity declined into a dark age of poverty, famine, pestilence, and war that lasted for 1000 years.

Finally, in Italy and throughout Europe, the Renaissance began.Trade expanded, inventions poured onto the market, the printing press was invented, and a new age began.

Instead of looting and plundering, and ceaseless wars, people organized into cities, provinces, and states, formed guilds, developed skills, initiated trade, discovered the Americas, and began creating and producing products and wealth at a rate never seen before.

The Affluent Society

On the crest of this revolution of thought and incredible advancements in science and technology, the American nation was born, rooted in the fundamental principles of life, liberty, and the pursuit of happiness.

The Constitution and the Bill of Rights were designed to create a legal structure to assure that the United States would be a nation where anyone could come and build a life free from oppression and expropriation.

The concept of "making money," of creating wealth and keeping ownership of it, was revolutionary. For more than 200 years, up to the current day, people have flocked from all over the world by the millions to participate in this American dream. Because of the E-Factor programmed deep into human nature, America, like all countries, has its crime and corruption. But fortunately,America is the first country to be governed from the outset by law, rather than the arbitrary whims of people in power.

Protecting the People

The Founding Fathers realized that the greatest danger to individual freedom was the *government* and the tendency of people in power to use government action and coercion to get the things they wanted the fastest and easiest way possible.

To guard against this, the Founding Fathers set up a system of checks and balances to protect individual citizens against the government. They were determined to put in place a constitution that would assure that "government of the people, by the people and for the people" would prevail for the indefinite future.

For 200 years, and up to the current day, it was generally understood that you achieved financial success by producing goods and services of value, earning a good living thereby, and saving out of your income to provide for your future needs and your retirement.

The foundation principles of the American republic are *freedom, liberty, honesty, individualism, self-reliance, responsibility, courage, determination, and competition, all practiced within the framework of peaceful cooperation.*

The role of government in this system is to keep the peace, to protect citizens from external aggression with an army and navy and from internal threats to life and property with police and courts.

To assure maximum entrepreneurial activity, growth, and prosperity in the economic sphere, the role of government is to protect private property, enforce contracts, and maintain a stable currency.

As long as the government restricted its role to these few activities, America flourished and became the economic powerhouse of the world.

The Creation of Wealth

In the twentieth century, in America and throughout the more advanced, industrialized countries, incredible achievements in wealth creation produced a cornucopia of products and services never before imaginable, and still not imaginable in most of the world.

More wealth was created in a shorter time than ever before in history. Between 1815 and 1914, the living standard of the average person in America or England rose one hundred times! With this extraordinary growth in living standards and expansion of wealth and the wealthy, the E-Factor began to rear its ugly head. For the first time people began to believe it was possible to get *something for nothing*. Well-meaning people, dreamers, and utopians, with no understanding of entrepreneurship, risk, investment, productivity, capital flows, or competition, began to think in terms of "sharing" this newly created wealth.

Not understanding that everything has to be produced by the labor of someone, well-meaning people began promoting the idea that the government should use its powers to expropriate the wealth and property of the successful in order to share it with people they considered to be less fortunate or more deserving.

The Violation of Natural Laws

From then to now, the guiding principle of "redistribution" has been to violate the natural laws of *cause and effect, sowing and reaping, and action and reaction*. The idea of *something for nothing*, appealing to a few people at first, and then more and more, fed off the twin emotions of envy and resentment.

The dam began to break as the twentieth century progressed. Ideas for redistribution increased and multiplied without control or limit. Politicians eager for votes began offering "free money" in exchange for those votes, and many got elected. They promised to use the power of the law and the power of taxation, backed by the threat of fines, arrest, and imprisonment, to expropriate money and property from those who had produced it to give to those who had not produced it.

If what government began doing to the individual taxpayer was done by one private party to another, it would be called "theft." When done behind the veil of the law, it is called "policy" or "compassion." However it is defined, taking money away from those who have earned it to give to those who have not earned it, is a form of stealing. Once voters began to realize they could get "free money" by voting for the right person, the E-Factor was unleashed like a flood.

Every government *free money* scheme benefits one specific subset of voters while it penalizes another specific, usually smaller, subset of voters. For example, laws restricting apartment rentals are always aimed at penalizing apartment owners with the aim of benefiting apartment renters. There are always vastly more tenants than landowners. The E-Factor reigns supreme.

The Roots of National Insanity

As we know now, the idea of "free money" makes people crazy. It drives them insane. It quickly becomes an obsession. Free money releases passions and triggers behaviors that can lead to demonstrations and riots.

Urged on by demagogues and aided by the stench of envy, mixed with resentment, multiplied by greed for the property of others, justifications for national theft filled the air. The successful were called "robber barons" and disparaged on every street corner. The *something for nothing* people ignored the fact that it was the entrepreneurial energy, risk-taking courage, and inventiveness of people like Henry Ford, Thomas Edison, John D. Rockefeller, and Harvey Firestone, all of whom started with nothing, that created thousands of jobs while they reinvested almost everything they earned.

As the twentieth century progressed, the *something for nothing* fever raged like an epidemic, flowing into the Roaring Twenties and driving stock market prices through the roof. People began to believe there was no limit to the amount of free money they could get from government policies and programs, or unearned money from soaring stock prices.

The Bad Deal

But the party had to end, and so it did on October 26, 1929, with the Great Crash. Over the next two years, the stock market continued downward. The unemployment rate rose to 24 percent. The New Deal of Franklin D. Roosevelt failed completely. Instead of allowing the free market to exert its natural corrective influence on the economy, both Herbert Hoover and Franklin D. Roosevelt imposed sweeping regulations on wages and prices. The regulations, combined with the Smoot-Harley tariffs, crippled world trade and drove many other countries into depression as well.

Even though Franklin D. Roosevelt was hailed as a hero for his efforts, everything he did made the situation *worse*. Year after year, the unemployment rate was stuck above 20 percent. By 1938, almost nine years after the start of the Depression, the unemployment rate was up to 28 percent in the U.S. People began predicting the Depression would go on for decades and might never end.

World War II ended the Depression by absorbing hundreds of thousands of men and women into the factories and the Armed Forces. During World War II, as in all wars, the government grew and expanded, eventually controlling more than 40 percent of the U.S. economy. After the war, as normally happens, it never really went back to its former size.

The Golden Age Begins

In the 1950s, the greatest age of American prosperity began. America was the only country left unscathed by the war. Its industrial plant was intact. It had the capacity to produce more goods and services than all the rest of the world put together. The demand for American products was seemingly insatiable.

The primary reason for prosperity in the United States, then and now, was and is the innovativeness, productivity, and managerial excellence of American individuals and corporations, in comparison to and in competition with the rest of the world.

The Baby Boomers and the 1960s

However, in the 1960s the baby boomer generation began pouring out of the schools and universities and into the workforce. They had no memory of the Depression or World War II and no understanding of the sources of wealth and prosperity: hard work and productive corporations.

All they saw around them was prosperity. Professors like John Kenneth Galbraith, in his book The Affluent Society, declared that America had reached the point where wealth creation was inevitable and unstoppable. The only questions were, *"How do we control it, spend it, redistribute it, and give it away to those who need it?"*

In 1965, President Lyndon Johnson initiated his Great Society legislation and the E-Factor was unleashed. The desire to get something for nothing exploded. Every conceivable program for the War on Poverty was launched, eventually costing more than five trillion dollars, without reducing poverty at all. Today, the percentage of people officially living in poverty is very much the same as it was in the 1960s.

Free Money Sweeps the Nation

Year after year, in every state house and department in Washington, idea after idea, program after program, to distribute "free money"—to poor people, farmers, corporations, the old, the young, the sick, the well, and everyone in-between—was embraced. Politics became a means for using government power to tax, regulate, expropriate, and channel free money in all directions, but especially to targeted voters.

The new mantra of politicians, repeated over and over on Capitol Hill and throughout Washington, was, "Tax, Tax, Tax; Spend, Spend, Spend; Elect, Elect, Elect!"

The Electoral Auctions

Every election became an *auction* where the candidates competed to outdo each other in offering even more free money to their voter base. Government grew and grew. Taxes were increased, and increased some more. Politicians spent even more than they could tax and covered the gap with borrowings and printed money. This led to inflation, huge deficits, and multitrillion-dollar national debts that will never be repaid.

The idea of "free money" causes people to lose all sense of reality. They begin to believe impossible things, especially that there is no link between producing and consuming. They begin to believe there is a bottomless bucket of free money controlled by politicians that they are entitled to. The free money sickness soon became an obsession. People began to think of nothing else.

The Unintended Consequences of Free Money

But "free money," *something for nothing*, destroys the soul of the person who gets it, or who even tries to get it. It causes him to engage in crooked thinking and impossible rationalizations to explain why he is entitled to this free money.

Almost always, the desire to get or give free money is disguised by high-sounding talk about "the poor, the sick, the aged, or the young," all guaranteed to tug at the heartstrings of normal people.

In every case however, people either want free money for themselves directly, or they want to be in charge of giving free money to others as a source of employment or gratitude or both.

The Corruption of Free Money

Here is the problem. As Aristotle explained in his *Nicomachean Ethics,* *"The ultimate aim of all action is to achieve the happiness of the actor."* The core psychological requirement for happiness is a feeling of personal value and self-esteem, a condition in which you genuinely like and respect yourself.

But true and lasting self-esteem and happiness are only possible when you feel you are making a *contribution* to your world that is greater than the amount that you are receiving back. When you feel what you are doing is important and valuable, and that you are doing more than you are getting paid for, you feel good about yourself.

However, if your aim is to take money away from those who produce it to give to yourself or others, you are engaging in a form of *theft* that actually diminishes the well being of everyone affected.

People who *receive* free money or benefits that they have not earned, feel angry, diminished, dishonest, and of lower value. Their feelings of insecurity increase, and their self-esteem plummets.

Most people at the receiving end of government "free money" programs are neither thankful nor grateful. Instead they are more likely to be sullen and demanding. The fastest way to trigger an angry demonstration or a series of vituperative television ads is to threaten to reduce or even modify the free money or privileges going to a favored group.

The Free Money Addiction

Free money is like an addictive drug. From the first taste, like crack cocaine, the recipient of free money is *hooked*. Once he has taken it for a while, he must have even more to get the same temporary satisfaction. No amount is ever enough.

Addiction to free money, whether as a welfare recipient, criminal, or person who lives off the sweat of others, leads to feelings of resentment, hostility, insecurity, and ever escalating demands for more free money. Today, our entire society is infected with this *something for nothing* virus, corrupting all our social and political systems.

In every government office, people are lined up to ask for, demand, plead for, beg for, and protest for more free money. The only obstacle to the complete collapse of our society into a political war of all against all for more free money is the bulwark of law that underpins our society, and the character of the men and women who refuse to succumb to the siren song of *something for nothing*.

Two Major Motivators

There are two major motivators of behavior that modify and affect the basic instincts and desires we discussed in Chapters One and Two. The first is the *desire for gain*. This is extremely intense and a major motivator, whether it is for *safety, security, leisure, comfort, love, respect, or fulfillment*, and especially if its focus is *power and money*.

The second major motivator of behavior is the *fear of loss*, of having something taken away. According to psychologists, the fear of loss is at least two and a half times more powerful than the desire for gain.

What this means is that people are strongly motivated to get what they want the fastest and easiest way possible, preferably free. But if you threaten to take something they already have away from them, their motivation to protect and defend what they have is at least two and a half times more powerful.

Threatening to reduce or cut off people's free money or benefits from the government or any other source, triggers far more resistance and even violent behavior than they demonstrated to get the free money in the first place.

This intense resistance to the threatened withdrawal of free money or benefits explains why people pour into the streets to demonstrate and protest at any proposed reduction in government programs.

The Only Antidote to Free Money Sickness

The only cure for the E-Factor disease, aimed at *something for nothing*, is to not make it available in the first place.

Wherever *something for nothing* has taken root, triggering personal and emotional devastation, it must be cut back as quickly as possible lest the recipients be destroyed morally, ethically, and emotionally.

Remember, there is never an end to the justifications for legal theft via taxation, to reward and benefit those who have not earned it. But whenever you violate the natural laws of cause and effect, sowing and reaping, action and reaction, you set in motion a series of events with long-term consequences that are often vastly worse than if you had done nothing at all.

The Ongoing Contest

The contest is always between the two approaches: *"short-term pain for long-term gain"* versus *"short-term gain for long-term pain."* Just as the cruelest thing parents can do is spoil their children, thereby setting them up for a lifetime of frustration and disappointment, the cruelest thing we can do for the less fortunate among us is get them addicted to free money, thereby destroying all their hopes for the future. We must not allow this to happen; and where it has already occurred, we must make every effort to stop it.

Accurate Diagnosis

In medicine they say, *"Accurate diagnosis is half the cure."* In these first five chapters, you have developed a complete and clear diagnosis, or understanding of why people do what they do. You now know what everyone wants, how the structure of incentives determines the actions people take, and how important character is.

You now understand the evolution and origins of the dilemma we face, both individually and as a people, and how we got here. Let us now look at what is happening in government as the result of the *something for nothing* principle gone berserk.

> *"It is possible that the scrupulously honest man may not grow rich so fast as the unscrupulous and dishonest one; but the success will be of a truer kind, earned without fraud or injustice. And even though a man should for a time be unsuccessful, still he must be honest; better lose all and save character. For character is itself a fortune.."*
>
> — Samuel Smiles

Chapter Six

Government, Politics, and Power

*"The American Republic will endure until the politicians
realize they can bribe the people with their own money."*

— Alexis de Tocqueville

The United States is the greatest country in the world. America is a great country not only because of its political system, but mainly because of its people. America is good because Americans are good. Americans are the most generous people on earth, giving more money to charity nationally and internationally each year than any other country, and probably more than all the other countries in the world put together.

America is the most welcoming country in the world. America accepts more new immigrants each year than all the countries of the world put together. America has the strongest economy in the world. With only 6 percent of the world's population and 6 percent of the world's land mass, the United States produces 30 percent of the total gross world product out of a total of 194 countries. The Los Angeles area alone, if it were a separate country, would be the seventh largest country in the world economically.

Militarily, America is the most powerful country in the world. Its Army, Navy, Air Force, Marines, and Coast Guard are the best equipped and trained, and are made up of some of the finest and most competent fighting men and women on earth. They are a force in every corner of the globe.

But all of these are *secondary* reasons for why America is such a great country. America is a great country because it provides more opportunities and possibilities for the average person than any other country on earth, or than in history.

Four Goals of Mankind

There are four common goals of all people, in all lands, at all times. They are *first* of all, to be healthy and to live a long life. *Second,* people want to be in stable families and enjoy happy relationships with others. *Third,* everyone wants to do meaningful work that makes a difference, and be well paid for it. *Fourth,* everyone wants to acquire enough money to be financially independent at some time in his or her life.

We know by now that because of the expediency factor, everyone is *lazy, greedy, ambitious, selfish, vain, ignorant, and impatient.* We know that everyone is motivated to get as much as they can of *safety, security, comfort, leisure, love, respect, and fulfillment.* We also know that the fastest and easiest way for a person to get all the things he wants is to acquire *money* or *power* or both.

The truth is that, in America, it is more possible for more people to get more of all the things they want, including the "big four" above, than in any other country on earth.

As a result, people from every country on earth flock to the United States to participate in the possibilities of America. No other country can say that. The American Green Card, allowing a person to live and work legally in the United States, is the most valuable and valued piece of paper on earth.

Greatness by Design

The United States of America is no accident. It was carefully designed in a constitutional convention containing some of the finest minds that have ever come together in a single place in the history of man on earth. The Declaration of Independence, the Constitution, and the Bill of Rights combined the best thinking of these remarkable men to create an exercise in self-government and democracy that had never been seen before. They combined the finest ideas man had ever thought and written about, from the first democracy of ancient Greece all the way through to the great thinkers of the Enlightenment, and created the American system of government, the longest enduring constitutional government in the world.

From the very beginning, the U.S. was designed for the common man, for the person starting with little or nothing, for the immigrant who came to America with little more than a hope and a dream. No other country on earth can make this claim. All the other countries were designed by and for the rich and powerful.

Our legal and commercial system was designed to encourage and reward *self-reliance, entrepreneurship, and personal responsibility.* It was based on the assumption that free men, living and working together within a framework of law and order that protected their rights to "life, liberty, and the pursuit of happiness," could and would create good lives for themselves and their neighbors.

The Lurking Danger

In the Federalist Papers, James Madison wrote and warned about the dangers of "factions." These were defined as individuals and groups who, driven by the E-Factor, by the normal human tendencies toward *laziness, greed, ambition, selfishness, ignorance, vanity, and impatience* aimed at the never-ending desire to achieve more *safety, security, comfort, leisure, love, respect, and fulfillment,* expressed in the desire for money and power as the fastest way to achieve them, might try to take advantage of others in society.

The chief concern of the Founding Fathers was to protect the individual citizen from the power of the government. Their intention was that the federal government should be small and limited. The state governments, closest to the people, should handle all but the functions that were only possible for the national government. They wanted to keep governments small at all levels because they knew that the power to tax and regulate is the power to harass and destroy. They had already experienced the abuses possible by government, in the form of unjust and unreasonable laws imposed on the colonies by the British government of King George III.

Checks and Balances

The key to maintaining maximum liberty and opportunity for Americans, which they only arrived at after many days and weeks of debate, was a system of *checks and balances.* The main purpose of these checks and balances was to block the government from infringing on the basic liberties fought for and won in the Revolutionary War.

Because the individual states were jealous and protective of their rights, the power of the central government was strictly *limited* to protecting national security and providing services in areas that individual states could not provide for themselves, such as armies and navies for national defense.

The primary role of government was designed to be the protection of the nation from *external* aggression and the protection of individual citizens from *internal* oppression, aggression or crime. All powers not specifically granted to the government by the people were to remain in the hands of the people. Power was handed up, rather than down.

A New Way of Governing
In the legal systems of England and the countries of Europe, power flowed downward from the king through representatives to the people. In the United States, however, the power was vested in individual citizens and was meant to flow from the people to their representatives and upward to the state houses, the Congress, and Senate. Power would flow from the individual states to the federal government. All powers not explicitly grant- ed to the federal government in the Constitution were to be the exclusive property of the states and only exercised by them.

Elected officials were to be selected by their neighbors to rep- resent their interests in the state house or in Washington. Running for and serving in office was looked upon as a civic duty, a contribution that one made to his country during the course of his career. Legislators were citizens with careers and businesses at home, to which they would return after having served their time in office. The Founding Fathers did not envi- sion career politicians who attempted to stay in office for the rest of their lives.

Government Has No Money
It was well known and generally understood at the founding that government had no money of its own. *Government produces nothing.* It only consumes. Every dollar that government gives out, it must first take away from someone in the form of taxes.

For every service that government performs, it must first tax the money away from *someone.* It then charges a minimum of

50 percent for administration before turning the money around and sending it back out to its chosen constituencies.

For every job that government creates, it must destroy at least one job in the private sector. It must eliminate a job that someone is doing to provide a product or service someone wants in order to create a government job doing something few people want, or at least, that no one is willing to pay for.

Whenever government builds a public building, you can be sure there is a private building, or more than one, that will not be built. Frederic Bastiat, the French economist, once wrote a booklet, "What Is Seen and What Is Not Seen." In this classic treatise, he points out that what government does with tax money is seen by the population, but what is "not seen" is the devastation caused by the money being taking away from people who have earned it, the jobs and businesses that are destroyed, and the hopes and dreams that are shattered.

Taxes and Regulations

The power to tax and regulate were hotly debated and jealously guarded at the founding and during the Constitutional Convention of 1787. The idea of an income tax was fought and resisted by members of both parties because of their fear that, once it was in place, it would be misused, manipulated, and continually increased. In fact, when the first income tax was passed by a constitutional amendment in 1915, it only called for a 1 percent tax on people earning $5000 or more ($100,000 in 2005 dollars). By 1920, tax rates had risen to 70 percent on some people, and virtually everyone in America was subject to income tax. As soon as the *something for nothing* dam broke, the spread of taxation became a flood.

Nonetheless, because of exemptions and deductions, in 1940 the federal government was only taxing away 11 percent of national income. Today, governments at all levels consume 42 percent of the national income, starting with income taxes on individuals and corporations and then extending to hundreds, if not thousands, of taxes and hidden charges at every level of society and on every imaginable product and activity. In 2004, the average person had to work until May 25 just to pay his taxes.

Driven by envy and resentment, and the need to get votes to create new taxes and raise existing taxes, opportunistic politicians always promise only to tax "the rich." Violating the basic American value of *equality*, which includes the tax laws, progressive taxation was introduced and then made more progressive each year.

In 2004, according to the IRS, the wealthiest 1 percent of taxpayers paid 33.89 percent of all federal income taxes. The wealthiest 5 percent paid 53.25 percent of income taxes. The top 10 percent paid 64.89 percent, the top 25 percent paid 82.90%, and the top 50 percent paid 96.03 percent of all federal income taxes. The bottom 50 percent of income earners in America paid only 3.97 percent of the taxes and consumed most of the services provided by government! And the only solution politicians have is to "tax the rich" even more.

Perhaps the height of dishonesty is when politicians say that reductions in tax rates, "only benefit the rich." Simple logic says that if you are making a high income, any general tax reduction will be more beneficial to you than to someone who pays no taxes at all. Reducing taxes only benefits people who are paying taxes in the first place.

Today in America, there are more and more people who pay little or no taxes at all who are voting for politicians who promise to give them more and more free money, to be paid out of taxes to be raised on those people who are already paying 96.03 percent of those taxes.

Tax and Spend

The purpose of government in general has become to *tax and spend.* Almost every piece of legislation and activity of government is aimed at taking money from some members of society and giving it to others. The goal of taxers and spenders is to extract as much money as possible without killing the goose that lays the golden egg. Sometimes they are successful, sometimes not.

In the early 1990s, the Democrat-dominated Congress passed a law that vastly increased the taxes on new *yachts.* Their contention was that only "the rich" purchased yachts, and "the rich" would continue paying this tax because, after all, they had so much money.

What Congress did not realize is that the entire yacht-building industry on the Eastern Seaboard consisted of tens of thousands of specialized carpenters, tinkerers, sail makers, hull builders, electricians, plumbers, craftsmen, artisans, and others who work together in teams to build these boats.

When Congress increased the taxes on new yachts but not on old or imported yachts, yacht buyers throughout America simply stopped buying new boats. Instead, they kept or refurbished their existing boats or bought yachts from other countries.

Most of the yacht-building industry went bankrupt. More than 90,000 skilled craftsmen, most with no other skills or way to earn a living, were thrown out of work. The outcry was so loud that the legislation was repealed, but not until after having wreaked enormous damage on countless small towns and villages where yacht building took place and on the families of the blue-collar workers who were bankrupted in the interim. The law of unintended consequences had struck again!

Running For Office

Let us now look at the process of acquiring and using political power. When a person begins to think of running for office, his personality, values, and convictions often change, sometimes dramatically. No matter what his ideas and principles, clear or unclear, before declaring for office, as soon as potential voters begin questioning him he begins backing and shuffling, double talking and speaking out of both sides of his mouth.

Politicians are essentially *entrepreneurial* in nature. They are going into the market to sell a product, themselves. The payment they are seeking is the votes of the electorate. The electorate chooses their representative based on the relative attractiveness of the "package" the candidate offers. Every single principle of marketing and sales, determined by pollsters, consultants, and advisors, is brought to bear to win the political prize. After all, enormous amounts of money can be at stake.

The Foundation of Political Principles

James Buchanan, Jr., 1986 winner of the Nobel Prize in economics, received his award for his work in "Public Choice Theory." In his exhaustive research, he demonstrated that political expediency, the desire of *lazy, greedy, ambitious, selfish, vain, ignorant, and impatient* people to get elected to office so they can get the *power, perks, and money* that office provides, would determine what positions these people would take to get elected. Buchanan proved that *opinion polls* on various issues taken in the politician's district were a better and more accurate predictor of the politician's platform and programs than any other economic, social, or philosophic principle.

In other words, most politicians running for office say what they need to say to attract the greatest number of potential voters to help them get elected the fastest and easiest way possible.

Because politicians are human, we should not expect them to behave otherwise. Neither should we be surprised when they act like typical politicians. That's what they are.

The Thought of Winning

Something happens to a person when the smell of power gets into his nostrils. His personality changes. The idea of "winning" distorts his valuations. The thought of being elected is exciting and stimulating. He soon comes to believe that winning is not just the only thing; *winning is everything.*

Joseph Lieberman has been in the Senate for many years and is one of the most thoughtful and respected politicians in Washington, on both sides of the House. But when Al Gore selected him as his running mate in 2000, within twenty-four hours he had abandoned most of the principles he had espoused all his political life. He did a complete reversal to embrace the far-left positions of Al Gore.

As soon as the election was over and the Gore-Lieberman ticket had lost, Lieberman went back to his position in the Senate, picked up his tattered principles, and began espousing them once more. But for a brief shining moment, he became totally expedient, as politicians almost always are when their election or reelection is at stake.

The Reality of Running for Office

The first thing that happens to a politician when he decides to run for office is that he is confronted with the fact that politics is *highly competitive*, like an entrepreneurial marketplace. In most cases, there are lots of other capable, determined people who also want to "serve" in office.

In too many cases, people running for office do not have much to run away from. They are usually trying to get away from lives and careers that are neither successful nor satisfying. They run for office seeking something outside of themselves to commit to and believe in. They are looking for something that will give them a sense of meaning and purpose that their current lives do not. Since everyone is seeking meaning and purpose in life, there is nothing wrong with this. It is neither good nor bad. It is just a fact of life. The only time this creates a problem is when people expect politicians to be other than they are.

Big Political Payoffs

For many candidates, the income they can receive in office is substantially more than they can earn in the private sector, and often more than they have ever earned before. For example, even the most mediocre legislator in the California state government earns more than $100,000 per year, plus all kinds of benefits and perks. Most of these people have never seen that kind of money in their lives.

The pension plans for elected officials, usually kept as quiet as possible from the electorate, are extremely generous. Often they amount to hundreds of thousands of dollars, and even millions, in pensions over the course of a politician's lifetime. Sometimes, a politician only has to serve *one term* to qualify for thousands of dollars per month for life.

One of the most important concerns of people in office is to pass laws and regulations that assure they will be well provided for when they leave office. As Mark Twain once said, *"We get the best government that money can buy."*

Show Me the Money

To get elected, and to be *expedient*, politicians often abandon ideas they have espoused all their lives. Once they get into office, put there by the donations, support, and work of people who espouse certain ideas and want certain pay-offs, the politician has to deliver.

Once elected, the politician finds himself in league with other politicians of his party, and often with members of the other party, all who have promised rewards and favors to the people who elected them. It becomes immediately clear that there is not enough *free money* to go around. Compromises will have to be made. Some people will have to be paid off immediately, and some later.

To get anything done, to have any influence, a politician has to engage in the twin exercises of "back scratching," which means working cooperatively with other politicians, and "log-rolling," which means supporting the promises of others in order to get support for his promises to his voters.

The Never-Ending Grabbing Match

In every case, alas, politicians get elected by offering some variation of *something for nothing* that will benefit their supporters. This is most common in the left wing, Democratic, socialistic parties, the members of which are mostly convinced that anyone who is successful deserves to have their money taxed away from them for the benefit of others.

Sometimes politicians get elected by promising to *defend* individuals and groups against the *something for nothing* hoards that throng the state houses and Washington. Occasionally, they get elected by promising to cut off the free money going into some group, like the out-of-control Workman's Compensation scandal in California in 2004. (Not only were costs three times the identical system of benefits offered by Arizona, with most of the money going to lawyers, chiropractors, doctors, and uninjured workers, but the amounts actually being received by genuinely injured workers were among the lowest in the nation.)

The only honorable reason to run for office is to work for legislation that rewards and encourages people to save, invest, and produce the wealth that our society depends on for growth and opportunity. It is to encourage entrepreneurship on the one hand and to reduce the tax burden and weight of regulation on the other.

The honest politician works to allow individuals to keep more of their hard-earned money and to reduce the number of people caught in the trap of government dependency. The good politician does everything possible to protect the private citizen or corporation against the free money crazies that get elected to power.

The Four Stages of Power

Throughout the ages, the acquisition and maintenance of political power has gone through four stages. What the politician does and how he behaves is determined by the stage he is in at the moment.

In stage one, the entire focus of the politician is to *acquire* the power in the first place. This electioneering often requires Herculean efforts and a pretzel-like twisting of principles to satisfy enough voters to gain him a majority and get him into office in competition with others seeking the same position.

In the second stage of power, the politician has to *hold onto* the power, increase it, and consolidate it. Since most politicians have no other means of support, their security in office becomes a primary need and motivation. Once elected, the politician must do everything possible to form alliances and coalitions with other politicians so he can deliver the goods and fulfill his promises to his voters.

Defend and Consolidate

In the third stage of power, the politician has to defend his power from those who want to take it away from him or from those who competed against him in the first place. Power in politics is a *zero-sum game*. If some people get it, other people have to lose it. There is therefore a never-ending contest among elected politicians to trade power and favors back and forth in order to achieve their own personal goals and simultaneously frustrate their rivals, the fastest and easiest ways possible.

The politician must also defend and protect his power from people in the other party who are determined to do everything possible to block the politician from rewarding his voters, for obvious reasons.

Demonize the Opposition

In this process of defending his hard-won office, the politician soon begins to "demonize" the people who disagree or resist his exertion of power. This demonizing of the opposition happens when the politician makes the leap of thinking from his winning the election to the conclusion that the *reason* he won the election was because he was better and his ideas were superior to those who also wanted, or still want, the office.

The politician then goes a step further and concludes, "If I am better, which has been proven by my electoral victory, then my opponents must be worse." The politician then assumes that if he is right, his opponent must be *wrong*. If he is *good,* his opponent must be bad. Howard Dean, defeated Democratic candidate for the presidency and head of the Democratic National Committee, summarized this in his reference to Republicans, *"This is a battle between the forces of good and evil, and we are the good."*

Saints versus Sinners

Finally, the politician reaches the stage of self-justification and self-defense where he concludes that anyone who disagrees with him is a "bad person." Once he has characterized his opponents as "bad," he can then justify punishing them or their supporters with taxes and regulations or by giving free money and benefits to his supporters that must be paid for by the supporters of his opponents.

In the highly partisan political world of today, politicians of each party see the members of the other party as bad, evil, destructive, and harmful to the body politic. They see themselves as saints, ordained to slay the dragons of the other party. They see themselves as having the duty and responsibility to block or frustrate their opponents in every way possible.

Reelection Is Everything

The fourth stage of political power is *getting reelected*. It is in this stage that the E-Factor surges to the top and dominates all political advertising, campaigning, and political positioning. The common saying in politics is, *"If you're not in office, you're nothing!"*

James Buchanan Jr. proved in his Nobel Prize thesis that, in most cases, a politician's desire for reelection, for retaining power, becomes an obsession that dictates all other considerations.

In Washington recently, a Democratic politician explained it this way. He said, *"The reason that I say things about my opponent that may not be true is simple. If my opponent loses, he has a job and a career to go back to. If I lose, I don't eat."*

Under these circumstances, which person will be the most likely to engage in electoral activities that might be questionable later? When election or reelection is at stake, some politicians, especially the *something for nothing* people, will say anything or take any position to get into or back into office. They have very few prospects in the private sector.

The Reasons for Political Power

There are two main reasons for wanting to acquire political power, or any power for that matter, aside from the rewards and benefits of office.

The first is the desire to give *free money* to particular constituencies by taxing it and expropriating it from others. This type of power is guided by pure expediency. The politician whose primary goal is to give money away to others is intensely *lazy, greedy, ambitious, selfish, vain, ignorant, and impatient.* He is determined to use every skill possible to achieve his goal of power so he can get more of the *safety, security, comfort, leisure, love, respect, and fulfillment* that he intensely desires. This politician will do anything to get and keep power. He will abandon any principle, betray any friend, backtrack on any position, and reverse himself wherever he perceives it can be helpful.

When this politician runs for office, he will be like a bidder at the electoral auction, offering voters promises of free money and benefits that are to be taken from someone, usually unnamed, who has earned it, and to be given to some group who has not, but who is expected to vote for the politician.

The Long-Term Thinker

The second reason that a person desires power is rooted in the qualities of the character of the politician. He will be focused not on personal aggrandizement or getting *something for nothing* for a selected voter group but on achieving goals and benefits for the general populace over the long term. The honest politician focuses on introducing policies and programs that tap into the expedient nature of people to engage in economic and social activities that increase prosperity, opportunity, and growth for the greatest number of people.

It has been said that a *politician* is a person who thinks about the next election; but a *statesman* is a person who thinks about the next generation.

Expediency-based politics is aimed at short-term gain (immediate votes) for long-term pain (higher taxes, more regulation, and lower living standards).

Character-based politics is aimed at short-term pain (reduced taxes and smaller government) in exchange for long-term gain (increased incentives for growth, opportunity, and prosperity).

The Law of Duality

In politics, as in many areas of life, the Law of Duality prevails. This law says, *"There are always two reasons for doing something, the real reason and the reason that sounds good."*

The reason that sounds good is always the emotional appeal to give free money to "the young, the old, the sick, and the poor." The "real reason" however is that the fastest and easiest way to get the votes a politician needs is to offer free money to the greatest number of people and groups. It is to appeal to the lowest common denominator of human compassion, combined with an insatiable desire to get or give *something for nothing*.

History as a Guide

For 2000 years, societies have grown and prospered to the degree to which men and women of principle have fought for and introduced policies aimed at long-term prosperity for their societies, always against the bitter resistance and antagonism of people who want free money *now*.

Throughout history, virtually every society that has reduced taxes and regulation and encouraged entrepreneurship, thereby making it expedient for people to save, invest, and produce, has prospered, sometimes almost overnight. After World War II, both

Japan, completely destroyed, and India, emerging from being a colony of England, started with very little. Japan, with no natural resources, introduced a free market, capitalist system while India, loaded with natural resources, imposed nationwide socialism. Twenty-five years later, the average standard of living in Japan was one hundred times that of India!

The lower, flatter, fairer, and more transparent the taxes, the more hope and opportunity there will be for more people, and the more incentive there will be to take risks, start businesses, and create wealth and jobs. On the other hand, the higher, more progressive, more complicated, and unfair the tax system (the U.S. tax code now runs more than 44,000 pages, and no one really understands it), the greater the drag on the economy and the bleaker the long-term future for the children and the little guy starting out.

Incentive-Based Economics

The very best and most prosperous society is one that orients every tax, regulation, and policy so that it flows in harmony with the E-Factor.

Every policy and law must be designed so that people, seeking the fastest and easiest way to get the things they want with the least concern for the secondary consequences of their actions, are motivated to engage in those actions that create wealth, prosperity, and opportunity for more people.

Boobs and Bureaucrats

Why is it that government is so corrupt, wasteful, and inefficient? It takes about three times as many people to do the same job in government as in the private sector. It takes several times as long to do the job, and almost invariably the result is a lower level of quality.

The way to understand why government cannot do anything particularly well is to look at the "structure of incentives" in government. In the private sector, people have to get results or they get fired. In the government sector, no results are required. A completely ineffective, inefficient government department, program, or employee can go on for years, with ever-increasing budgets and staff, without ever achieving any results at all. There are no incentives for excellent performance, or for any performance.

Scientists Discover New Element: GOVERNMENTIUM

A major research institution has just announced the discovery of the heaviest element known to science. The new element has been named "Governmentium."

Governmentium has one neutron, 12 assistant neutrons, 75 deputy neurons, and 224 assistant deputy neutrons, giving it an atomic mass of 311.

These 311 particles are held together by forces called morons, which are surrounded by vast quantities of lepton-like particles called peons. Since Governmentium has no electrons, it is inert. However, it can be detected as it impedes every reaction with which it comes into contact.

A minute amount of Governmentium causes one reaction to take over four days to complete, when it would normally take less than a second.

Governmentium has a normal half-life of four years; it does not decay but instead undergoes a reorganization in which a portion of the assistant neutrons and deputy neutrons exchange places. In fact, Governmentium's mass will actually increase over time since each reorganization will cause more morons to become neutrons, forming isodopes. This characteristic of moron-promotion leads some scientists to believe that Governmentium is formed whenever morons reach a certain quantity in concentration. This hypothetical quantity is referred to as "Critical Morass."

When catalyzed with money, Governmentium becomes Administratium, an element which radiates just as much energy since it has half as many peons but twice as many morons.

From "Joseph Judge"

Government Employees Are Expedient

Every person, including those who work for government at any level, is expedient. He is *lazy, greedy, ambitious, selfish, vain, ignorant, and impatient.* Each government employee wants the same things. He wants to get more and more of *safety, security, comfort, leisure, love, respect, and fulfillment.* Government employees always seek the fastest and easiest way to get these rewards, with little concern for the long-term consequences of their actions. Each government employee is focused, all day long, on acquiring and holding on to *money* and *power.*

The incentive system in government is *perverse.* People do not get paid for getting results but for increasing the size of their departments and budgets. The pay scales in government are determined by how many people and how much money you control. There is a built-in pressure at every level of government to grow. Almost every government department applies for increases in its budget every year. This is why Ronald Reagan said, *"The closest thing to eternal life on earth is a government program."*

Bureaucracies Have Their Own Rules

Some people say that government bureaucracies and private-sector bureaucracies are the same. This is not true. In government, the bureaucracy is designed to follow instructions, to comply with orders, to carry out policy directives. It is forbidden to be creative or innovative, or to deviate from its instructions in any way. No matter what the external pressure, government bureaucracies function at their own speed (slow) in the process of performing their tasks.

In a private-sector bureaucracy, someone is always responsible for results. There are specific performance measures in place. If the job is not done quickly and efficiently, people are replaced. Private-sector bureaucracies have clear, specific targets that they must meet, along with budgets and schedules that are continually scrutinized to find ways to operate more efficiently.

Highly Talented, Motivated People Need Not Apply

People who go to work for government, aside from political appointees, are not particularly talented or competent. The government tends to attract the less capable members of the workforce. As an example, when there was a temporary government shutdown in the 1990s, fully 90 percent of government workers were classified as "non-essential." What this meant was that it did not matter whether or not they came to work on a particular day. They were told to remain at home until the budget impasse was resolved.

One of the protests you hear whenever there is a suggestion that a government department be cut back or closed down is that the people working there are "otherwise unemployable." It is generally assumed that if a person is ejected from a government job, he will be unable to find a job anywhere else. This is partially true.

The worst piece of information a person can have on his job application form in the private sector is a long period in a government job. In the private sector, it is automatically assumed that if a person has worked for the government for any period of time, he is probably lazy and inefficient. Why else would he have stayed with the government?

The New Elite

For many years, up to the 1960s, government employees earned about 10 percent less than similar positions in the private sector. This was offset by giving them higher levels of job security, one of the basic human needs, especially for people who are not particularly highly skilled. In addition, they received excellent medical care and a good pension plan. After thirty years of government service, a person could retire with a good pension that would enable him to live comfortably for the rest of his life.

Today in Washington, and in the states, there are many individuals and couples who will work for thirty years, from age twenty to fifty, and then "retire" after qualifying for their pensions, payable for the rest of their lives. The next day after "retiring" they will move sideways into another government job that pays the same or more than they were earning before "retirement" and in effect, have a second income for as long as they work. This is called "double dipping" and is both popular and common in government work at all levels. It is neither possible nor allowable in the private sector.

The New Deal for Government Employees

In 1960, John F. Kennedy, who actually lost the election to Richard Nixon except for last-minute ballot box stuffing in Illinois, was desperate for every vote. He promised to give government employees the right to unionize, which they never had before, if they would support his candidacy. They did and he did.

From the 1960s on, unionization in every industrial sector in the United States has declined dramatically, down from 33 percent in 1955 to about 11 percent today. But unionization has continued to grow throughout the public sector, finally including virtually every single person who works for government at any level. Once the unions had organized government employees, the E-Factor exploded into government activities.

Union officials, who are *lazy, greedy, ambitious, selfish, vain, ignorant, and impatient*, all eager to get the *power* and *money* that would enable them to have more of the *safety, security, comfort, leisure, love, respect, and fulfillment* they want, began demanding more and more for their members.

Today, government workers are some of the most coddled, cared for, and privileged people in our society. They have been called the "new elite." Once they get a government job they go onto the "never, never, never get fired plan." It is almost impossible to remove them for any reason. Today, it takes two full years and more than $200,000 worth of legal costs and administrative hearings to get rid of one incompetent or dishonest government employee. For most senior people in government, it is not worth the trouble.

The Six P's of Government Employment
Government employees, because they can never be fired and because there are no standards or demands set on them for job performance, are completely focused on the six P's. These are Pay, Perks, Privileges, Position, Power, and Pensions. From morning to night, government employees think about how they can get more and more of the six P's, faster and easier, with no concern whatever for what is likely to happen as a result of their behaviors.

Some people will say that "all government employees cannot be like that; there must be some good ones." The author Damon Runyon once wrote, "The race is not always to the swift, nor the contest to the strong, but that's the way to bet." There are definitely some wonderful, competent, dedicated, hard-working men and women of character in government service, but because of the structure of incentives, they have almost no chance to make a meaningful difference.

You Can't Buck the System
Government employees are allowed to "tinker" with problems but never to solve them. If ever a government employee solves a problem or finds a way to reduce expenditures in his area of responsibility, he is immediately chastised by his superiors and by the union. It is not uncommon for government unions to get

people demoted or even fired who work hard and do a good job. This kind of excellent performance "reflects badly on the others."

In addition to the hundreds of thousands of government employees, all motivated by expediency, all determined to keep their jobs, supervised and managed by people who feel the same way, there are thousands of commissions and boards, both nationally and at the state level. These thousands of government-appointed groups are packed with the husbands and wives of politicians, as well as the donors and supporters of their campaigns. These people sometimes earn tens of thousands of dollars of *free money* per year, and often hundreds of thousands of dollars, for attending meetings a few times a year.

Government Grows Like Weeds

Government is very much like crabgrass. It needs no encouragement to grow. It is almost impossible to root out. Left to itself, it continues to expand until it actually chokes out private-sector activities. Like a cancer, it kills healthy cells and begins draining the financial energy of the country. It requires more and more money and personnel to perform more and more functions at an increasingly lower level of quality.

When New Zealand began to implement "Rogernomics," the government sold off, closed down, and gave away hundreds of government-owned corporations and departments. The amount of the gross national product of New Zealand going to government dropped from about 60 percent to 29 percent in five years. The government got out of virtually everything and turned most of it over to the private sector. As a result, the following year New Zealand was rated as the "least corrupt country in the world."

The reason for this was that there was so little government largess or patronage left to hand out. Instead of going to government seeking undeserved handouts, people just went to work in the private sector. The economy boomed.

What Is to Be Done?

What can be done to deal with the corruption, inefficiency, and waste in government at all levels? Some politicians are trying to cut it back. But the resistance from public-sector unions is intense.

When Stephen Goldsmith became the mayor of Indianapolis a few years ago, the city was on the verge of bankruptcy. Costs were out of control and city services were deplorable. He ran on a campaign of "Cleaning up the Mess."

The first thing he did was to apply the "Yellow Pages Test" to every city government activity. Whatever it was, he would open the Yellow Pages. If there were three or more companies that offered the same service that a government department was offering, he threw the service open for bidding. City unions were allowed to bid on the same level playing field as private companies.

Initially, the civil service unions went *ballistic*. They wept and cried about the terrible suffering that would befall the people of Indianapolis if the unions were not in charge of various services. But to no avail. The contracts were thrown open.

Unions Are Entrepreneurial Too

When the unions realized that they had no choice but to compete with private sector companies, they quickly reorganized themselves. The Expediency Factor works in *both directions,* both for good and for ill. They sat down with their people and made major changes. They got serious about keeping their jobs.

All by themselves, they began to cut back on waste and inefficiency. They moved people around and put the most competent people in the most important jobs. In many cases, they won the initial bidding against the private-sector companies and carried out the job with unexpected quality and efficiency. If they did not win the bidding, they were given a short period of time to reorganize or the department was shut down. Within a couple of years, Indianapolis had its budget under control and its city government running efficiently and effectively. The citizens were delighted.

Competition Makes Things Better

Competition is the key. When there is no competition, inefficiency, corruption, and waste thrive, especially in the realm of government. As soon as competition is introduced, people acting expediently have to quickly upgrade their skills and streamline their activities if they want to continue getting the *safety, security, comfort, leisure, love, respect, and fulfillment* that is so important to them.

Bureaucrats, unions, and incompetent people *hate* the very idea of competition. Because they are expedient, because they are *lazy, greedy, ambitious, selfish, vain, ignorant, and impatient,* because they always strive to get the things they want the fastest and easiest way possible, their first reaction to the suggestion of competition is always wails of protest, demonstrations, and every political manipulation possible to sabotage the idea.

Based on the E-Factor, they have discovered that protesting and complaining are the *fastest and easiest ways* to block any change that might cause them to have to work *harder* to get the things they want. Whenever you see or hear about protests or demonstrations, you can know for sure that organized groups are attempting to intimidate weak-kneed politicians into protecting their flow of free or easy money.

Competition or Quality?

Without competition, quality declines, costs skyrocket, few results are achieved, and the situation becomes progressively worse. The deplorable level of government services in Russia under communism is just one of many examples of what happens when there is no competition for the *safety, security, comfort, leisure, love, respect, and fulfillment* that everyone wants. The poor quality of most government services in the United States is another example people experience every day.

Sometimes people say that government "must be made more efficient." This is impossible. People who work in government think all day long about how they can "game the system." Like water flowing downhill, through every hole and crevice, they continually seek ways to get the things they want faster and easier, with no concern for what might happen in the long run.

Someone once said, *"You cannot make anything foolproof, because fools are so ingenious."* They will always find a way around any attempt to improve government services.

Peter Drucker, the management expert, once wrote, *"The only thing that you will always have in abundance is incompetence. Systems must be designed so that incompetent people working together can still get the job done properly."*

This is accomplished by structuring the system in such a way that completely expedient people have no other choice but to do the job well, on time, on budget, and to an acceptable level of quality.

Fix It or Shut It Down

The only way to end corruption, inefficiency, waste, and mismanagement in government is to either introduce competition for the six P's, for the money and power, and the *safety, security, comfort, leisure, love, respect, and fulfillment* that each person is striving for, or shut down the department altogether. Tinkering at the edges never works.

Any other solution to the problem of the size and inefficiency of government except by radically altering the structure of incentives is both dishonest and disingenuous. It is self-serving and almost always aimed at getting something for nothing for someone. The cure for the out-of-control size and cost of government is to cut it back, reducing activities to only those that are indispensable and cannot be done by private individuals and organizations at a profit.

We can start by looking in the Yellow Pages.

"Badness you can get easily, in quantity: the road is smooth, and lies close by. But in front of excellence the immortal gods have put sweat, and long and steep is the way to it."

— Hesiod

Chapter Seven

The Foundations of the American Dream

"Whenever you see a successful business, someone once made a courageous decision."

— Peter Drucker

In a free market economy like the United States, the customer is king or queen, and the E-Factor rules supreme. Business and entrepreneurship are devoted to serving customers, to improving the lives and work of ordinary people. This is what makes the American dream possible.

In a free society, it is not what companies produce, but what customers want and need that determines economic activity. The most successful businesses are those that most accurately identify the wants of customers and then satisfy those wants with products and services that customers are willing to buy and pay for.

As Calvin Coolidge once said, *"The business of America is business."*

From the first "Yankee" peddler through to the present day, the United States has been a business-centered country. Starting with an unexplored continent, all wealth from then to now has been created, rather than inherited as in the European countries.

The Structure of Incentives

The structure of incentives in America is strongly oriented toward the encouragement of productive business activities. The foreign policy of the United States, going all the way back to the years immediately after the Revolutionary War, has always been to engage in activities ultimately beneficial to the American business system.

Productive individuals and businesses produce all wealth. Successful business activities ultimately provide all jobs. Excess revenues generated by businesses pay for all roads, schools, hospitals, and governments. As Winston Churchill once said, *"Free enterprise is the sturdy horse that pulls the wagon in which everyone rides."*

The Sparkplug of American Prosperity

The *entrepreneur* is the sparkplug in the engine of the free market and the business system. It is the entrepreneur who recognizes or anticipates a customer need, then assembles the resources necessary to satisfy that need at a price that yields a profit. It is this ability that creates all wealth and opportunity.

The first principle of economics is *scarcity*. An economic good is, by definition, one that is limited in supply or availability. There is not enough of it to satisfy everyone who wants it. At the same time, individual desires and needs are *unlimited*. The only thing that is limited is people's ability to acquire more of the things they want.

Competition is the most powerful factor influencing the free market. There are numerous entrepreneurs seeking to get the things they want the fastest and easiest way possible. In a market society, however, you can only prosper by serving customers faster, better, and cheaper than your competitors.

The structure of incentives in the free market rewards innovation and creativity in the competition to serve customers better, faster, and cheaper. It brings out the best in each person who enters the market to compete for customers.

Entrepreneurship Is Risky

Entrepreneurs are those who take risks to produce goods and services for customers, gambling that the customers will be there to pay prices high enough to yield a profit. These profits are essential for the entrepreneur to repeat the process of developing and producing even more products and services in the future.

Customers are expedient. They are *lazy, greedy, ambitious, selfish, vain, ignorant, and impatient.* They seek *safety, security, comfort, leisure, love, respect, and fulfillment,* the fastest and easiest way possible. Businesses and businesspeople only succeed if they satisfy these customers faster, better, and cheaper than their competitors.

Starting and building a successful business, based on catering to demanding, disloyal, impatient customers, is hard work, fraught with risk and peril and the constant threat of losses rather than profits.

According to the Small Business Administration, fully 80 percent of new businesses go broke, close up, or shut down in the first two to four years. According to *Forbes* magazine, from 1900 to 2000 more than 82 percent of the "Fortune 100," the largest and most successful companies in America, closed down, went bankrupt, or were acquired by other companies. Only eighteen survived.

The Companies of Tomorrow

Some of the biggest and most profitable companies in America today, such as Microsoft, Dell, Oracle, and Apple, did not exist twenty-five years ago. Each year, new companies emerge and older companies disappear. The process of "creative destruction" in the marketplace never ends.

Customers' wants and needs are changing continually, like the weather, from one day to the next, from one week, month, or year to the next. They never remain the same for very long.

All business activities are aimed at riding the wild horses of thousands and millions of expedient customers to produce and deliver products and services where, when, and how customers want them, at prices they are willing to pay.

It is customers who pay all wages and benefits. As Sam Walton once said, *"Our only boss is the customer and he can fire us at any time he wants just by shopping somewhere else."*

Business is where the E-Factor runs rampant in the most positive and beneficial way. Everywhere you look, in every business activity, promotion, or advertisement you see greedy, ambitious, clever people and companies striving to sell the very largest quantity of products and services at the highest possible prices to the greatest number of customers. And this is a good thing.

The Customer Benefits the Most

Because of competition and consumer choice, these lazy, greedy, and determined business-people have no option but to continually improve their offerings to make them more attractive and desirable than those of their competitors.

Meanwhile, those lazy, greedy, and impatient customers always have three choices: First, they can buy what a particular company offers; second, they can buy something another company offers; and third, they can refrain from buying anything at all.

In a free market, all choices are *voluntary*. A person only enters into a voluntary exchange when he feels he will be better off as a result of the exchange rather than if he had not entered into the exchange at all. This means that before he will buy something, the customer must value the benefits of the product or service more than he values the amount of money it costs and more than any other benefit or satisfaction available to him at the same time for the same amount of money.

The Dynamics of the Free Market
The free market is the vast national and international meeting place where buyers and sellers come together to negotiate and decide what to sell, what to buy, at what prices, and under what terms.

As the result of unfettered customer choice, combined with the desire of businesses to prosper, millions and billions of buying and selling decisions are made each day.

The result of this never ending, turbulent market activity is that capital, labor, and resources are constantly allocated and reallocated efficiently in pursuit of customer satisfaction.

The "bright side" of the free market is when businesses strive to please customers in the short term while simultaneously thinking about and planning for the long term. The best businesses are those dedicated to building and maintaining customer loyalty so that once they sell something to a customer, the customer is so happy and satisfied that he or she buys again and again.

The Dark Side of Business
The "dark side" of business occurs when lazy, greedy, selfish people offer shoddy or disreputable products or services aimed at achieving a quick gain, with no concern for the long-term consequences for either themselves or their customers.

Fortunately, the principle of *caveat emptor*, "buyer beware," is so deeply ingrained in the thinking of customers today that companies that do not satisfy their customers in the short term quickly go out of business.

It is a general rule in advertising that you *"never promote a poor product."* The reason for this is simple. If you promote a poor product, people will buy it. If people buy it and are dissatisfied, they will not only refrain from buying it again, but they will tell others that the product is no good. This is why advertising a bad product will kill the product in the marketplace faster than anything else you can do.

Customer Satisfaction Is the Prize

The market is a vast, complex contest with one prize over which businesses compete—*customer satisfaction.* The principle of "free enterprise" says that, *"the more enterprising you are in serving other people, the freer you are as well."*

The free enterprise system allows anyone with an idea to serve people better to enter the market and compete. In America, most people start off with little or nothing. Most fortunes begin with the sale of personal services and grow out of savings and profits.

In addition, most new products and services *fail,* at least in their original forms. The difference between government and business in this area is important. If government launches a program that is unsuccessful, usually because it attempts to get people to act other than expediently, it increases the budget and staff of the program to try to make it work. If an entrepreneur fails with a product or service, he must quickly revise it to make it more satisfying to customers, take it off the market, or go broke.

Competition Brings Out the Best

To succeed in a competitive market, many of the very best qualities of the individual are demanded. At a minimum, a successful entrepreneur requires *courage*, both to begin in the first place and persist against endless problems and disappointments.

An entrepreneur requires *honesty and integrity* to win the support of customers, suppliers, employees, and sources of capital and finance. As ex-IBM president Lou Gerstner said in his book *Who Says Elephants Can't Dance?*, *"No one should be entrusted to lead any business or institution unless he or she has impeccable personal integrity."*

In addition, an entrepreneur must be optimistic, energetic, visionary, determined, intelligent, flexible, and able to bounce back repeatedly from disappointment and temporary failure.

An entrepreneur, above all, requires an *instinct* for identifying what products or services he or she can produce and offer that extremely demanding customers will buy and pay for.

Because of the E-Factor and the drive to get things faster, better, and cheaper, a successful entrepreneur is forced to develop these vital human qualities at a high level if he or she wants to survive and thrive.

The Enemies of Free Enterprise

Large, established businesses are not fans or friends of free enterprise. They see young, upstart companies as threats to their markets and their very existence. Large companies see small companies as constantly seeking ways to lure their customers away with lower prices or better services.

Because of the E-Factor, if large companies can manipulate the political system to get special privileges, subsidies, tax breaks, or place import duties on competitors, they will always do it. In his book *Money for Nothing,* Fred S. McChesney points out that companies will make financial contributions to politicians in exchange for special favors. The amounts they will pay in "campaign contributions" are based on careful calculations of the increment of profit that those businesses expect to receive from the special favors. They are pure business decisions.

Follow the Green

Every piece of legislation affecting business *benefits* someone and *penalizes* someone else. Politicians are expedient, as we already know. They respond to incentives, just like everyone else. They need "campaign contributions" in order to get reelected. They are *lazy, greedy, ambitious, selfish, vain, ignorant, and impatient* to get and keep the power and money they desire. They recognize that the primary source of their power is the special interest groups who give them money in order to get special privileges they cannot or will not earn in the free market by satisfying people in some way.

The key to understanding business and politics is to *"follow the green!"* Always ask the two questions, *"Who benefits?"* and *"Who pays?"*

Every limitation, tax, regulation, or restriction on business of any kind creates a winner and a loser. Unfortunately, the loser is almost always the consumer, the little guy, who wants to get the very most for the very least, just like everyone else. The key to understanding political activity is to identify exactly who the winners and losers are and how much regulation is involved.

The Free Market Works Best

Here is the bottom line: because of the natural instincts, "A," and common desires, "C," of all people, the free market is the most ideal, "B," for producing the greatest quality and quantity of products and services at the lowest prices for the greatest number of people. The free market is the most effective form of a completely spontaneous system of "non-organization" ever imagined in all of human history.

In the free market, the entrepreneur initiates and drives all innovation and improvement in the service of satisfying customers, not out of altruism or generosity, but because of the E-Factor.

Each society is successful to the exact degree to which it supports, encourages, rewards, and promotes entrepreneurs and entrepreneurial activity. According to *Fortune* magazine, each year about 8 percent of companies and jobs disappear by natural attrition. To grow economically, a city, state, region, or country has to replace these companies and jobs, plus create even more, to maintain the same level of economic activity and offer opportunities to new members of the workforce.

Each time taxes are lowered, regulations are removed, and operating costs of a new business are reduced, business activity increases. The natural, spontaneous desires of individuals driven by the E-Factor to improve their situations causes entrepreneurs to emerge naturally, like grass growing after a spring rain.

The ten states with the lowest taxes and regulations in the United States have growth rates that are double those of the ten states with the highest taxes and regulations. To grow economically, all a state has to do is to slash taxes and bureaucracy and make it more attractive to locate a new business in that state rather than somewhere else. What is it about this that politicians don't understand?

The True Wealth of Nations

In America today, according to the OECD in Paris, 11.9 percent of the working population are entrepreneurs, more than in any other industrialized country. Fully 19 percent of the working population today is working in companies that are less than forty-two months old.

Small companies create 70 percent of the new jobs. They are

forming at the rate of more than two million new businesses per year.

Most people can work at a job once it is created, but only 10 percent to 12 percent of the population has the ability to create companies and jobs.

Entrepreneurs and business builders are the true *national treasures* in any country. They create the future with their imagination, energy, and daring. They are the primary source of hope, growth, and opportunity for most people. In addition, fully 80 percent of self-made millionaires, the "rich," got there by starting and building their own businesses, creating jobs and wealth for numerous people in the process.

Government's Role in the Economy

Because of the E-Factor and the central role of new business activity in creating jobs and wealth, serving customers, and generating revenues, the primary role of government should be to *stimulate* entrepreneurship. Government should teach and encourage entrepreneurship, reward and praise entrepreneurship, and make entrepreneurship the central focus of economic and social policy. Government at all levels should go through every piece of legislation, existing and proposed, and ask, *"Does this stimulate the starting of new businesses or not?"*

The central economic policy focus of government should be to remove any barriers to entrepreneurship that may exist today. Every act of government to create the climate of incentives that induces people to start and build new businesses will help all businesses at every level. By unleashing the incredible energies of entrepreneurship, the U.S., or any nation (think about Hong Kong, Taiwan, Singapore, and Korea), can increase wealth, expand job opportunities, and achieve all economic and social goals.

Strength of Will

When John F. Kennedy asked Werner Von Braun, the head of the American Space Program, what it would take to put a man on the moon, he replied simply, "The will to do it."

What the U.S. needs today is a new birth of liberty expressed in a national commitment to promote entrepreneurial activity by removing the hindrances that hold it back. Because of the E-Factor, entrepreneurial activity within a framework of law, supported by lower taxes, minimum regulation, and an absence of government interference, will spontaneously create jobs, hope, opportunity, and prosperity for more and more Americans.

All that is required is "the will to do it."

"Opportunities? They are all around us....There is power lying latent everywhere waiting for the observant eye to discover it."

— Orison Swett Marden

Chapter Eight

Working for a Living

"The only security a man can ever have is the ability to do a job uncommonly well."

— Abraham Lincoln

How on earth did so many people get the idea that they are *entitled* to a well-paying job? Even worse, where did people get the idea that somehow government is responsible for creating these jobs? How is it that people who have made no effort to upgrade their skills for years can suddenly be upset and angry when no one will pay them the kind of money that they want to earn?

There is no place where the E-Factor and the desire to get *something for nothing* come together as powerfully as in the world of work. Too many people who work want to get paid more and more for doing less and less, and they are constantly amazed when they meet resistance to this from every corner.

Most People Are Lazy

Most of our problems with employment are caused by the fact that most people don't want to get up on Monday morning and go to work. Most people are lazy. They will only work if they see that there is no other way to get the things they want. But they don't have to like it.

One of the most pressing responsibilities for any business is to make the work interesting, challenging, and rewarding. It is to match the interests and abilities of the individual with the requirements and responsibilities of the job. It is to do everything possible to encourage people to want to come to work and do a good job.

Nonetheless, the first basic needs of each person are for *safety and security*, especially financial security from a steady job. Once these needs are fulfilled and a person feels secure in his work, these needs have limited motivational power. You can only motivate a person who has satisfied these needs by threatening to take them away.

As soon as a person is assured of job security, the next needs he has are for *comfort and leisure*. Once people have a job, they want to take it easy, to work as little as possible for their pay. They are expedient. They want to get the very most for the very least. They are *lazy, greedy, ambitious, selfish, vain, ignorant, and impatient.*

The 80/20 Rule at Work

The 80/20 Rule seems to apply to the world of work. About 20 percent of people enjoy their work, want to do more of it, and do it better. They view success in their work as an important part of the fulfillment of their own unique personal potentials. These people soon rise to the top in any company of value and become the key people around which all business activities are organized.

According to Robert Rector and Rea Hederman Jr. of the Heritage Foundation, people in the top 20 percent tend to perform five times as much labor as those in the bottom 20 percent. There are nearly five hours of paid work performed in the

Census top 20 percent of income earners for every hour of work performed by people in the bottom 20 percent of income earners.

On the other hand, the lower 80 percent of income earners consider their work to be a necessary evil, something they have to do to earn the money to support their lifestyles. In many respects, these people see their work as a punishment, something they have to endure, a penalty they have to pay to enjoy the rest of their lives. People with this attitude have a very limited future.

The bottom 80 percent of people in the workforce seek to do the very least amount of work possible while continually demanding to be paid more for it. These people are the source of all problems and complaints in the world of work. They are the reasons for defective work and poor quality. They are the ones who drive away customers.

Labor Is a Commodity
The greatest problem with regard to work is that most people do not understand how their jobs fit into the great scheme of things. Labor is a *commodity*, like any other factor of production. An employer pays a certain amount of money in exchange for a certain quality and quantity of work. This quality and quantity of work is then combined with the work of others to produce a product or service that can then be sold in the marketplace at a profit.

Labor is usually the most important and costly factor of production, but it is nonetheless just a part of the overall production process.

Each person considers his individual labor, physical or mental, to be something unique, personal, and special, an expression of his life and personality.

But everyone else, including employers and customers, views the work of others as a *cost of production*. Being expedient, both employers and customers seek for the best and cheapest products and services possible, including the lowest labor cost possible.

Because people view labor as a variable cost, acting expediently, they strive to reduce that cost in every way possible. It is not personal. It is just business.

Competition Determines Wage Rates

For businesses, lowering costs for any factor of production, including labor, which is typically 65 percent to 85 percent of the cost of any product or service, enables them to compete more effectively by lowering prices, or it enables them to earn higher profits, or both.

In a free market, the worker voluntarily agrees to accept a particular job in exchange for a particular amount of money. All things considered, both employee and employer expect to be better off as the result of this exchange, or it wouldn't take place.

In the private sector, the employer works for the *customer.* The customer demands the very most for the very least. The employer must satisfy this demand or be put out of business by someone who will.

Customers pay all wages, salaries, and benefits, not employers. Employers merely collect the monies needed to pay for the costs of production, including labor, by selling products and services in sufficient quantities at sufficient prices.

When individuals, driven by expediency, need a job and the money that accompanies it, they make every effort to sell their labor at the highest price possible. The employer, acting *for the customer,* who demands the lowest prices, attempts to hire the necessary labor components of the products and services he produces at the lowest possible price. This is how wage rates, salaries, and incomes are determined.

People Like to Take It Easy

Once a person has a job and feels relatively secure in that job, he then moves up the hierarchy of needs to *comfort* and *leisure*. He then does everything possible to enjoy more comfort and leisure at work.

According to Robert Half International, fully 50 percent of working time today is wasted, mostly in idle chitchat with coworkers, personal business, and extended coffee and lunch breaks.

As I mentioned earlier, the average workweek in America today is thirty-two hours, even though most people are paid for forty hours. Not only is much of that time wasted, but the time when the employee is actually working is often spent on low-priority tasks that contribute limited value to the employer.

The History of the Labor Movement

Unionized labor activities are usually the worst example of the "dark side" of the E-Factor in action at work. This has been true from the very beginning of the history of organized labor.

For thousands of years, the life of the average person was "nasty, brutish, and short." In Europe, right up into the 1700s, there were an average of *seven* famines per century in which millions of people perished from hunger. People slaved away seven days a week in the countryside, working on small plots, paying taxes to the landowner, and just scraping by year after year.

Then in England, with the invention of the Spinning Jenny, the first machine to spin yarn out of cotton, the Industrial

Revolution began. Each new invention and advance in production technology enabled individuals and organizations to produce more and more with less labor, at lower costs.

The growing demand for labor to operate the new machinery attracted thousands of people from the farms into the cities to work in the mills and factories. It was a time of the greatest social and economic turbulence in human history, and it still goes on today in developing countries. Throughout the developing world, people continue to move from farms and villages into the bigger cities seeking opportunities for better work and higher pay.

Terrible Working Conditions

Working and living conditions at the beginning of the Industrial Revolution were terrible. People were required to work twelve to fourteen hours per day, seven days per week, with no more than a couple of days off each year for Christmas and Easter. Nonetheless, people flocked to these jobs from all over because they were vastly better than the ghastly conditions they had experienced working on the land.

In the midst of this social turmoil, the British Parliament legalized the first "Working Man's Association" in 1820. The organizers of these associations immediately proclaimed that their goal was to shut down British manufacturing and stop the introduction of new labor-saving machinery. Recognizing this as a threat to growth and prosperity, in 1824 Parliament revoked these rights and shut down the movement.

For a brief period during the 1820s, the followers of a labor revolutionary named Ned Ludd and his "Luddites" roamed across England attacking factories and destroying machinery. They somehow had the idea it was the machinery that was causing the appalling working conditions in the factories and mills, and if the machinery was destroyed, peace and social harmony, which had never existed in the first place, would somehow return. They were soon arrested and jailed, but their legacy lives on today.

Some Things Never Change

When unions were finally legalized again in England in 1870, forty-five years later, their first order of business was to establish *monopolies*, similar to the old guild systems, to protect the jobs of their members. This was achieved by blocking the entry of new people to a particular factory or industry for fear that competition from these hungry laborers would drive down the wages of people already employed.

Some things never change. Today, the aims of most union activity are the same three things: first, unions continually demand more money and benefits for less work; second, unions demand control over the workers who are allowed to be employed in the business or industry, thereby keeping their own wages higher by blocking competition from workers who are willing to take the job for less than "union scale." Third, unions continually fight to block the introduction of new technology that will lead to increased productivity and lower costs. If this judgment seems harsh, just look at any union contract or study the demands in any union-management negotiation. Better yet, look at the reasons unions give for any strike or threat to strike. They are almost always one of the three reasons given above.

Everyone Suffers Eventually

Politicians seeking the votes of unionized workers and the campaign contributions of the unions that represent them, continuously conspire to block competitive imports, subsidize inefficient union-based industries, and force employers to pay "union scale" (read: excess wages) to anyone employed doing unionized work or government subsidized work of any kind.

Expediency reigns supreme. The *first* victims of excessive union wage rates are the customers who have to pay more for union-made products, often of lower quality.

Being expedient however, customers soon start buying lower-cost products and services from non-unionized companies or from overseas suppliers where wage costs are lower.

The *second* victims of the union movement are the unionized workers themselves. They may get higher wages in the short term, but in the long term their jobs gradually disappear and they end up out on the street, starting over with obsolete skills.

The *third* victims of the union movement are all other workers who are forbidden to work in union-dominated industries and who then have to accept lower wages or get jobs with non-unionized companies who are shut out of bidding for jobs or contracts. Everyone loses.

Excess Wages Destroy Industries

Today, the heavily unionized steel industry is an ongoing tragedy of insolvency, bankruptcy, and the permanent laying off of tens of thousands of workers, never to work again in that industry.

The airline industry is going through a wrenching readjustment as the major carriers, saddled with enormous union wage costs and work restrictions, are pushed to the edge of bankruptcy by lower-cost carriers.

The automobile industry is forced to close plant after plant, laying off tens of thousands of workers permanently as production and jobs gravitate to non-unionized Japanese and German manufacturers or migrate to Mexico.

Meanwhile, the non-union juggernaut Wal-Mart has become

the biggest company in the world by continually offering "Everyday Low Prices." Every single person in Wal-Mart, from the president to the new employee, is committed to offering quality products at the lowest possible prices, treating their customers with courtesy and respect throughout. As a result, customers who want to get the very best and most at the lowest price buy from Wal-Mart to the tune of billions of dollars each month.

You Can't Get More For Less

There is no such thing as *something for nothing*. It is not possible in the long run for anyone to be paid more money for doing less work. It is not possible to permanently charge more for labor than the employee contributes in value. In the final analysis, each person reaps exactly what he sows, no more and no less.

The solution to each person's desire for a good job at high wages is to continually upgrade his or her skills, getting better and better at doing more and more of those things employers value most and customers are willing to pay for.

What Determines How Much You Earn

In the world of work, you will always be paid in direct proportion to three things: first, the work you do; second, how well you do it; and third, the difficulty of replacing you. Your responsibility is to choose the right job for your special talents and skills, become very good at doing that job, and then make yourself *indispensable*. This is the key to your future.

We live in a free society. Each person is *responsible* for his own life and work. Each person is responsible for acquiring and developing the skills necessary to earn the kind of money he wants to earn in the current, continually changing marketplace.

Each person is responsible for continually upgrading his skills so he can do what people are willing to pay for today.

The True Source of Well-Paid Jobs

Opportunistic politicians, labor leaders, demagogues, and activists are often heard demanding that somehow "the economy must create more higher-paid jobs." However, there is no such thing as "the economy." There are only millions of expedient individuals acting in their own best interests to get the things they want the fastest and easiest way possible.

You regularly hear some politicians demanding that other politicians do something to "create jobs." But politicians have no ability whatsoever to create jobs. All they can do is to create the economic climate that encourages risk-taking entrepreneurs to invest in the production of goods and services people want, and in so doing, create jobs for the people necessary to produce those products and services.

An investment of private savings is required to create a job. In retail, a business might invest $50,000 in buildings, equipment, computers, furniture, stock, and training for each job created. In manufacturing, it might cost as much as $500,000 to create a single job. All this money is *risk capital*. It is a gamble. It must come out of someone's pocket. It is invested as speculation with the hope, but not the guarantee, that it will eventually earn a profit.

Individuals Create Their Own Jobs

Here is a key question. Who is really responsible for creating a highly paid job? The answer is that *only* the individual worker, by making himself more productive and valuable, can create a higher paying job for him or herself. No one can make another person more productive. A company can only create an environment where a productive person can utilize more of his potential to contribute value. But the individual is always personally responsible for his level of production and the amount he earns or fails to earn.

You Are the Boss

The worst mistake you can ever make is to ever think you work for anyone else but *yourself.* In a larger sense, we are all self-employed, presidents of our own personal services corporations.

From the day you take your first job until the day you retire, no matter who signs your paycheck, you are the *president* of your own entrepreneurial business, selling your services into a competitive, constantly changing marketplace. Your company has one employee, *yourself.* As the president of your own personal services corporation, you are totally responsible for training and development, productivity and quality control, personal promotion, and financial management.

This attitude of self-employment requires the total acceptance of personal responsibility for one's life. And this is not optional. The fact is that each person is *already* responsible for himself, and for everything that happens to him. The only difference among people is that some people are aware of this and some are not. But everyone is responsible for their own lives.

Getting Paid More

You are where you are and earning what you are because of *yourself.* Wherever you are in life, whatever you are doing, however much you are being paid, you have chosen it yourself by your actions and even more so by your *inactions.* You have gotten to where you are as a result of the things you have done and the things you have *neglected* to do. If you are not happy with your work or your income, you must make new choices and decisions and take new actions. You're in charge.

If a *company* wants to increase sales and profitability, it seeks out new markets for different products or services or seeks to offer better and more attractive products and services in its existing markets.

As a self-responsible *individual*, you are in charge of upgrading your skills and abilities and becoming a more valuable, productive person in your field. This is the only way to create a high-paying job.

If you want to earn more money, find someone who is *already* earning more than you and find out what they did to get there. Follow the leaders, not the followers. By the Law of Cause and Effect, if you do what other successful people do, you will eventually get the same results they do. And if you don't, you won't.

Three Factors Driving the Economy Today
There are three factors driving our economic system today: information explosion, technology expansion, and competition. The amount of information available is doubling every two or three years. Technological expansion is taking place worldwide and is accelerating. Competition drives the growth of information and the introduction of new technology. Each multiplies times each of the others.

To compete in the world of work today, each person must be continually learning new subjects, mastering new technologies, and finding ways to meet and beat the competition for your job, both nationally and internationally. There is no other way.

Because of the *something for nothing* entitlement mentality, too many people are waiting around expecting things to get better, expecting jobs to somehow be "created" while they do nothing. The truth is, however, *your life only gets better when you get better.*

Job Skills Get Out Of Date Quickly

The cause of many of our labor problems is that too many people are not equipped with the knowledge and skills that employers want, need, and are willing to pay for in today's market. They are not equipped to perform the tasks necessary to produce the products and services that customers want at prices that customers are willing to pay. They have allowed their skills to become obsolete.

The solution for getting and keeping a high-paid job is for each individual to make a lifelong commitment to learning and maintaining the skills required to make a valuable contribution to serving current customers.

There are no dead-end careers. There are only individuals, who are responsible for their own lives and futures, who are not yet capable of doing a better job that people want, need, and are willing to pay for. The grass is not *greener on the other side*; it is greener where it is watered.

Unemployment Is Unnatural

Unemployment is an unusual and unnatural state of affairs. It does not exist in nature. There is always work to be done. Imagine putting a person, responsible for his own survival, on a desert island. Can you imagine his being "unemployed" for any period of time?

There are always unsolved human problems and unmet human needs. There is never any reason for any person to be unemployed at any time, except by *choice* or by government coercion, when government makes it illegal or unattractive to work.

All a person needs to do to get back into the workforce is do one or more of *three* things: first, lower the amount he is asking to perform a particular task. Offer to work for less. Second, do something else that people are willing to pay for. Third, move to a place where his current skills are in greater demand.

Offer a Better Package
To get back into the workforce, you simply have to offer an employer a competitive package, a combination of knowledge and skill at a lower price than you might have received in the past. During boom periods, some people earn amounts that are vastly in excess of what they are truly worth in a normal economy. When the economy comes back down, these people find themselves unemployed. To get back to work, they have to ask for a more realistic set of rewards.

The course of "creative destruction" eliminates industries and jobs. Customers no longer want the products and services produced by certain people and organizations. The advent of the automobile put horse and buggy manufacturers out of business. This is a normal, natural, and ongoing process in a market economy. If no one wants to hire you, even if you are the best *dotcom* programmer in the world, you must change your offerings and enter into a different labor market if you want to sell your "product," your personal services.

Government Created Unemployment
Long-term unemployment is invariably a government phenomenon. It is created and maintained by government policies. After the 1929 crash, Herbert Hoover, in a mistaken attempt to "help workers," ordered the government to freeze salaries and wages throughout the country, even though prices dropped by an average of 30 percent. Because employers were no longer free to

adjust their wage rates to the realities of a turbulent and declining market, they had no choice but to lay off workers by the tens of thousands and shut down their factories and plants. These inflexible wage rates prevailed throughout the 1930s, keeping the Depression going year after year.

Any attempt to interfere with the freedom of employers to pay what they want to pay or workers to work for whatever amount they agree upon leads to disruptions in the labor force, unemployment, and confusion in the minds of many people.

Minimum wage laws are a misguided attempt to *force* employers to pay amounts that unskilled workers are unable to justify at their current level of skills and productivity. They shut unskilled workers out of the labor force, slamming the door of opportunity in their faces. As economist Henry Hazlitt said, *"You cannot increase the value of a person's work by making it illegal to pay him less."*

There is no unemployment in places like Hong Kong where the maximum income tax is 15 percent and there are virtually no regulations on business or labor. In fact, there is a serious labor shortage, year after year. Companies cannot find enough people to take the incredible number of jobs that they continue to produce.

Jobs for Everyone

Any country could eliminate unemployment by simply applying the E-Factor to the world of work. First, make it *illegal* to fix any wage for anyone, under any circumstances, anywhere, in any business or industry. Allow wage rates to fluctuate freely. Allow anyone to go to work voluntarily for any amount that he is willing to accept. Allow employers to offer to pay any amount to anyone for any job. Wherever there is a completely free market in labor, everyone soon has a job where they are paid what they are worth in terms of their ability to contribute to the final product or service.

Second, kick the chair out from under the safety "hammock" that pays people so much for not working. Cut unemployment insurance payments in half and put a three-month fuse on them. In study after study, it has been demonstrated that many people remain unemployed until their unemployment insurance payments are just about to run out. In the last week or two before they get cut off, they suddenly and miraculously find a new job.

In 1996, when the government announced massive cuts in welfare payments and limits on how long people could receive welfare, millions of people got up from their couches and found jobs within a few weeks. Most of them never went back to welfare. The Expediency Factor wins again!

You Are Responsible

The key responsibility in the world of work for each person is to continually upgrade his skills and abilities and make himself increasingly valuable to a potential employer. It is up to each person to continually seek ways to contribute to the production of valuable products and services that customers want and need and are willing to pay for. As Henry Ford once said, *"The only real security that man will have in this world is a reserve of knowledge, experience, and ability."* This applies to everyone.

> *"If fifty million people say a foolish thing, it is still a foolish thing."*
> —Bertrand Russell

Chapter Nine

Law, Order, and Crime

"We cannot restore integrity and morality to our society until each of us—singly and individually—takes responsibility for our actions."

— Harry Emerson Fosdick

The power of expediency and the desire to get *something for nothing* is nowhere more obvious than in criminal behavior aimed at theft, fraud, embezzlement, or violence of some kind. As Thomas Jefferson wrote, *"The darkest day of a man's life is when he begins thinking about how he can get something to which he is not entitled."*

Richard Dawkins, the geneticist, in his book *The Selfish Gene*, theorized that everyone is genetically programmed to be selfish in assuring their personal survival, success, and procreation.

Many experts suggest that people also have a "criminal gene" that predisposes them to engage in dishonest behaviors, or as we would put it, attempting to get *something for nothing*. This theory says that almost everyone has the propensity to steal under the right circumstances. How many times have you heard the question, *"Would you do it if you were certain that you could get away with it?"*

We know now that this is the *something for nothing* impulse driven by the E-Factor, the fact that each person is *lazy, greedy, selfish, ambitious, vain, ignorant, and impatient.* This "criminal gene" is the manifestation of each person's desire to acquire *safety, security, comfort, leisure, love, respect, and fulfillment* the fastest and easiest way possible. It is rooted deep in human nature.

The Constraint on Dishonesty

Only a person with character, someone possessed of honesty and integrity that he or she will not compromise under any circumstances, can rise above and control this "genetic predisposition."

For too many others, the intense desire to get *something for nothing* impels them to rationalize and justify behaviors they know are anti-social and unacceptable. This is why they conduct them out of the sight of others whenever possible and *deny* that they have committed these crimes even when they are caught red-handed and in the presence of witnesses.

The Reason People Get Swindled

There is an old saying, *"You can't cheat an honest man."*

Every swindle and scam is aimed at people who can be tempted into believing that they can get back more than they put in, that they can get riches without working, that somehow, if everything goes just right, they can get *something for nothing.* The newspapers report stories every week of people who have lost their savings to crooks who have promised them huge returns on their money and then absconded with the funds. People seeking easy money are a criminal's favorite prey.

There is no "easy money." There is no way to get something for nothing. Get-rich-quick schemes only work for the perpetrator, not the victim. It's been said that, *"There's a sucker born every minute, and a con man born every 59 seconds to take advantage of him."*

Some time ago, a habitual criminal was released after serving most of his adult life in prison. When he was asked why he turned to a life of crime, he said, *"I did it for the easy money."*

The reporter asked, *"After all these years in prison, how do you feel about it now?"*

The criminal replied ruefully, *"Easy money was the hardest money I ever got."*

Hard Work and Patience Are Essential

It takes many years of hard work and experience to achieve success in any field. It takes many years of saving and investing to accumulate a financial estate. Most people do not start earning serious money until after the age of forty-five. It takes that many years to build up the reservoir of knowledge and experience that makes it possible for one to earn a substantial income. The average age of self-made millionaires in America is fifty-seven, and it takes approximately twenty-two years of hard work to get there. Mastery in any field, leading to high income, takes seven years on average and 10,000 hours of hard work. There are no shortcuts.

If anyone gets money quickly and easily, this money has to come from others who have acquired it slowly and painstakingly. The money has to be earned by someone before it can be stolen by someone else.

The Criminal Tendency

On the sliding scale of character that I described earlier, from ten (high) to one (low), the propensity to engage in criminal behavior increases as a person moves *down* the scale. People at the bottom of the character scale will steal at the first opportunity, almost reflexively.

In society, to protect against this type of person with this criminal instinct, there must always be a police power authorized to use force to stop criminal acts and a court system to punish them when they take place.

Civil society is only possible within a framework of law, order, respect for individuals and property, and a general commitment to the common good. Because of the criminal gene and the desire to get *something for nothing*, eternal vigilance is necessary.

The Only Cure for Criminality

Sadly enough, there are people who have little or no respect for law and order or for individuals and property and who do not particularly care about the common good of their fellow citizens. The only way to stop this type of person from engaging in criminal behavior is to arrest and incarcerate him.

Whenever there is no immediate threat of capture and punishment, criminal behavior happens spontaneously and automatically. The propensity to engage in theft and violence lies just beneath the surface in many people. It can be quickly activated by an opportunity to commit a crime and get away with it.

The South Central Los Angeles Riots

After the Rodney King trial in Simi Valley, in which the police were acquitted of brutality, people gathered in crowds in the low-income neighborhood of South Central Los Angeles.

Believing that the presence of the police might trigger negative reactions from the crowds, Los Angeles Police Chief Darryl Gates decided to withdraw all police from the area.

Two minutes after this withdrawal was announced on the

radio, the first window was broken and the full-fledged South Central riots and looting began.

For three days, South Central Los Angeles was in chaos, with buildings on fire and looters by the hundreds breaking into every store, carrying off food, furniture, television sets, and clothes.

Reporters from the major networks ventured in to cover the riots. When they asked rioters if they were looting because of their anger at the Rodney King verdict, fully 75 percent of the looters didn't know anything about it.

"Why are you rioting and looting?" the reporters asked. One looter, speaking for the majority of the looters, replied to the television cameraman, "Are you crazy? They ain't no cops!"

Three days later, the police were sent back into South Central Los Angeles. The looting stopped immediately. The riots ended. They never started up again.

In cities all over the U.S., crowds gathered to hear the Rodney King verdict. But the police never left those neighborhoods, and there was no rioting or looting anywhere, except in Los Angeles.

The point is that you can have all the crime you want in any society by just not punishing lawbreakers or by *not* punishing them quickly and visibly. You can reduce or even *eliminate* crime by making punishment swift and sure.

The *something for nothing* gene that lies just below the surface will explode into thievery and violence of all kinds as soon as the likelihood of punishment declines or disappears.

Criminal Behavior Involves a Choice
It is true that criminal acts may be triggered or exacerbated by poverty, drugs, alcohol, mental instability, external influences, and many other factors. These factors may be necessary, but they are not sufficient. Just because they exist does not mean that the person will commit a crime. Most poor people are honest.

Criminals in general, like most people, behave *rationally* in that they seek rewards versus punishment, success versus failure, easily gotten goods versus hard-earned success. This is the same even with better-educated, white-collar criminals. In other words, criminal behavior involves a *choice* on the part of the criminal.

This decision to commit a crime, like all occurrences, is subject to the Law of Probabilities. This law says, *"There is a probability that any given event will occur."*

Human beings, including criminals, are rational and calculating. They are *lazy, greedy, ambitious, selfish, vain, ignorant, and impatient.* They strive to get the *safety, security, comfort, leisure, love, respect, and fulfillment* they want in the fastest, easiest, and safest way possible. They commit crimes because stealing appears to be the best way to achieve their goals, all things considered.

Probabilities in Criminal Decision Making

According to criminologists, and based on interviews with convicted felons, there are four areas of probability that a criminal considers, consciously or unconsciously, before engaging in a criminal act. The first question the criminal asks is, *"Will I get caught?"*

What are the probabilities? Criminals fear arrest and incarceration more than anything else. If the probability of being caught is increased or decreased, the propensity for someone who is criminally inclined to commit a criminal act decreases or increases accordingly.

The second question a criminal considers is, *"If I am caught, will I be convicted and incarcerated?"*

If the probability of being caught is reasonably high and the probability of a stiff jail sentence, like a *three strikes* sentence, is high, criminal activities *decrease*. The "odds" are no good. In fact, once "Three Strikes" was passed in California, so many career criminals moved out of the state that California was accused of "exporting its crime problem."

If criminals are let off on *probation* more than once, they become even more likely to engage in criminal acts. The fear of incarceration, which serves as a deterrent to criminal behavior, loses its effectiveness.

An Economic Calculation

The third question the criminal considers is, *"If I get caught, arrested, and convicted, how much time am I likely to serve in jail or prison?"*

Because of the E-Factor, short sentences actually *increase* the propensity to engage in criminal activity. They actually increase the *demand* for criminal acts by inducing criminals to provide the *supply*.

According to Professor Joanna M. Shepherd of Clemson University, *truth-in-sentencing* laws, which require violent felons to serve up to 85 percent of their sentences, reduced violent crime rates. These laws reduced murder rates per 100,000 residents by 1.2 incidents. They reduced assaults by 44.8 incidents per 100,000 residents and robberies by 39.6 incidents. Rapes and larcenies also declined significantly.

A society that does not punish its criminals creates a market demand for more crime, not only by individual criminals, but by everyone they tell about how little time they served, if any.

Costs versus Rewards

The fourth question each criminal considers is, *"How much am I likely to steal and get away with in comparison with the amount of time I am likely to serve if caught?"*

The potential criminal then considers how long he would have to work to earn the same amount of money that he could get by stealing. If the amount of money he could get by stealing represents many months or even years of hard work and the likelihood of getting caught, arrested, and convicted is low, the structure of incentives favors engaging in criminal behavior.

According to Professor Stephen Levitt of the University of Chicago, for each prisoner released from prison, there was an increase of seventeen reported and unreported crimes per year. Every commutated death sentence was correlated with an increase of five murders. On the other hand, for each execution, on average, eighteen fewer murders occurred.

All these considerations blend into a simple decision, *"Do I commit the crime or not?"* This final decision will be the sum total result of the probabilities of the first four questions. This is easily provable by the experience of cities that post uniformed police officers in high-crime areas. The incidence of crime drops immediately.

Aiding and Abetting

One element that exacerbates this temptation to engage in criminal behavior is *criminal defense lawyers*. These people are also driven by the E-Factor, seeking the fastest and easiest way to get the *safety, security, comfort, leisure, love, respect, and fulfillment* they want. The fastest and easiest way to achieve their personal and financial goals is to get their clients off at all costs.

Most criminals have little money. They usually have to get out on bail so that they can steal enough to pay their legal bills, and criminal defense lawyers know this.

Repeat criminals have repeat needs for criminal lawyers. Every criminal lawyer knows that a criminal in jail is not a good source of income or billable hours. This is why criminal lawyers use every trick and technique possible to get their clients back on the street as soon as possible.

They Can't Help Themselves
We must accept that for some people at the lower end of the scale of character, criminal behavior is an immediate reflex to a criminal opportunity. This is why, throughout history, the only way to reduce criminality is by swift and sure punishment, combined with longer prison sentences.

Throughout the twentieth century, up to the 1960s, all forms of recorded crime in the U.S. decreased year by year. In 1960, the murder rate, for example, was just half of what it had been in 1934. During this period, policing was fast and efficient. Criminals were usually caught and arrested quickly and imprisoned with lengthy sentences. This rapid arrest and incarceration dramatically decreased the propensity of people on the margin to engage in criminal activities.

In the 1950s, the country was so safe that it was common for people to leave their keys in their cars and leave their homes unlocked when they went to work.

Encouraging Something for Nothing
In the 1960s, the baby boom generation, full of compassion and idealism, poured out of the universities with a popular new way of viewing criminals. Instead of seeing them as dangerous to themselves and society, they were viewed as innocent victims of poverty and other social conditions.

The Miranda Act gave more rights to criminals than ever before. Instead of catching a criminal and getting a quick confession, police were required to read the arrested person his rights: *"You have the right to remain silent. You have the right to a lawyer. If you cannot afford one, a lawyer will by provid-*

ed to you. Anything you say may be used against you in a court of law." This may have been justified by overly aggressive police work in some cases, but what it did was to give the arrested criminal ample time and opportunity to compose his story and deny guilt. This led to crowded courts, plea bargaining, release on bail, probation, and suspended sentences.

As it became *less likely* that a person would be caught, convicted, and incarcerated, the crime rate began to *increase.* Meanwhile, the length of jail sentences and even the probabilities of conviction *declined.* Many judges took great delight in throwing cases of obviously guilty criminals out of court on minor technicalities, such as a misspelling of the middle initial on the arrest report.

Predictably, crime rates rose continually throughout the 1970s and 1980s. Between 1960 and 1980, the national violent crime rate increased by 360 percent. The national murder rate doubled. The number of forcible rapes increased 380 percent. The number of robberies was up 420 percent. The aggravated assault rate increased 350 percent. The property-crimes rate, the burglary rate, and larceny-theft rate all jumped over 300 percent. America found itself experiencing a crime wave. People began saying that *"the criminal is back on the street before the victim is out of the hospital."*

The Tide Turns
Finally, in the 1980s the tide began to turn. Arrests and convictions increased. Mandatory prison sentences took the discretionary power of sentencing away from liberal judges who were releasing criminals on minor technicalities.

California passed its "three strikes" law, giving a three-time criminal a life sentence without parole. This law was a reaction

by voters to a criminal justice system that was enabling criminals to terrorize the population and even win lawsuits against
the victims who fought back.

As you can imagine, based on the E-Factor, the biggest foes of
"three strikes" laws and stiffer sentencing were the criminal
lawyers who were losing their paying customers one by one and
the politicians they were supporting.

An Act of Cruelty

The cruelest thing you can do to a person who is on the mental
verge of criminality is to tempt him to break the law by sug-
gesting that he can get away with it.

The perverse affect of coddling criminals, especially juveniles,
by granting probation, reducing sentences, and allowing parole
too early, is to encourage people of weak character, with little
self-discipline or self-control, to embrace a life of crime.

There is no better and more important place, based on the
ABC Formula of human behavior, for "tough love" than when
dealing with criminals, especially young criminals.

Alter the Structure of Incentives

The *primary* consideration of law enforcement at all levels must
be to protect law-abiding citizens. A society can have as much
or as little crime as it wants just by increasing or decreasing the
probability of punishment.

Unfortunately, people who deliberately set out to rob, cheat,
defraud, assault, rape, or murder innocent people understand no
other reasoning than rapid and effective law enforcement.

Swift and sure punishment is the only way to control the rate
of crime. It is the *kindest* way to organize society for the criminally inclined and especially for law-abiding men and women.

Most crimes in our society are committed by fewer than 5 percent of the criminals. According to a Justice Department study of state prisoners released in 1994, two thirds were rearrested within three years. In the meantime, these offenders had generated over 744,000 arrests, including 2,871 arrests for murder, 2,363 arrests for kidnapping, 2,444 arrests for rape, 3,151 arrests for other sexual assaults, 21,245 arrests for robbery, and 54,604 arrests for assault. Prior to their imprisonment, these prisoners accounted for 4.1 million arrests, including 550,004 violent-crime arrests.

The highest rearrest rates were for robbers (70.2 percent), burglars (74.0 percent), larcenists (74.6 percent), and motor vehicle thieves (78.8 percent).

These are the "hard core" criminals who are not capable of restraining themselves from engaging in criminal activities. They have fallen so far down the scale of character and human decency that they are virtually impossible to save. The only thing that can be done with them is to put them away for long periods of time, ideally beyond the criminally prone ages of fifteen to forty. Sometimes, considering the nature of the crimes, the very best thing a society can do is to incarcerate them for life.

The solution to criminal activity is to continually *raise the cost* of committing a crime until most criminal behavior is discouraged. It is to increase the likelihood of capture and long periods of incarceration until it makes no sense to the criminally inclined to risk such onerous punishment for such an unsure reward.

Organize the structure of incentives, based on the E-Factor, so that it makes more sense for more people to work for what they get and to become productive members of society.

Law, Order, and Crime

"The only true measure of success is the ratio between what we might have done and what we might have been on the one hand, and the thing we have made and the thing we have made of ourselves on the other."

— H.G. Wells

Chapter Ten

Welfare, Entitlements, and Society

"There are powers inside of you, which, if you could discover and use, would make of you everything you ever dreamed or imagined you could become."

— Orison Swett Marden

How did people ever get the idea that they could live off the hard work and sweat of others, and even worse, come to believe that they were entitled to take the food off of someone else's table to put on their own?

Welfare and all forms of unearned, undeserved free money stimulates and encourages the worst aspects of the E-Factor, driving more and more people toward seeking *something for nothing*. Free money destroys character and confidence, undermines self-worth, robs people of their dignity, and makes them feel like victims who have no control of their lives. And no matter how much free money they get, it is never enough.

You Have to Give Before You Get

For all the years of human history, up until about 1900, there was a direct, visible, and accepted link between sowing and reaping, between putting in and getting out. In the last one hundred years, throughout the industrialized countries, this link has been severed. Clever and complex government accounting procedures are now used to mask the fact that people are getting *something for nothing* to the detriment of everyone involved.

Opportunistic politicians, motivated to get votes by offering free money to more and more people, with fewer strings attached and fewer requirements, have driven the most powerful and prosperous countries in the world into technical bankruptcy.

According to economists, the total value of all land and property in the United States in 2005 is about forty-eight trillion dollars. However, the unfunded liabilities of Social Security, Medicare, AFDC, government pensions, and a thousand other government entitlement programs amount to over seventy-two trillion dollars. If the U.S. was a company, it would be declared insolvent and put into liquidation.

Using the numbers generated by Laurence J. Kotlikoff in his work on "intergenerational accounting," it is estimated that a child born today will be paying 76 percent to 84 percent of his or her income in taxes as an adult just to fund the entitlements on the books today. This assumes that there will be no more entitlement programs passed for the next *fifty* years. The latest Medicare program alone will cost more than seven trillion dollars that will have to come out of our taxes and taxes on our children.

No Long Time Perspective

For seventy-five years, since the 1930s, politicians of all types have been practicing the "après moi, le deluge" (after me, the flood) approach to political spending. The Social Security program passed in 1934 was actually a thinly disguised way of *increasing taxes* during the Depression. At that time, the life

174

expectancy of Americans was sixty-two years, so politicians set the age of retirement at sixty-five years. Thinking that they would never have to pay it out, they then spent every single penny collected every single year, up to the present day. With the retiring seventy million-strong baby boomer generation and a growing life expectancy of seventy-nine years, there are now at least $17 trillion of unfunded liabilities in Social Security. Where is this money going to come from?

Politicians of both parties have voted year after year to give increased amounts of money to more and more identifiable voting blocks, knowing that these amounts would eventually overwhelm the ability of the U.S. economy to pay them. But they weren't concerned. These politicians, with their incredibly generous pension and medical programs tied to inflation, would be out of office and retired long before the chickens came home to roost.

Trillions of dollars of debt have been heaped onto the shoulders of our children and grandchildren in exchange for current consumption for the current generation. These amounts can never be repaid.

The Grand Delusion

Where did people ever get the idea that they could spend money they did not earn? How did people come to believe that they could reap without sowing, consume without producing, live off the hard work and sweat of others? When and how did so many people come to believe that they were not responsible for themselves, for their lives, and for their own futures?

People are neither good nor bad as a rule. They are merely expedient. They are *lazy, greedy, ambitious, selfish, vain, ignorant, and impatient.* They continually seek to get more and more of the *safety, security, comfort, leisure, love, respect, and fulfillment* they desire. Whenever the prospect of free money, of *something for nothing* raises its ugly head, the ability of the average person to resist first weakens and then collapses.

Free money quickly becomes an addiction, as bad as any narcotic, distorting the senses, perverting values, weakening the recipient, turning him into an obsessed person who must have more and more.

No amount is ever enough. Like a drug addict, the recipient of free money needs more and more of it in order to be satisfied. If the additional supply of free money is not forthcoming, they demand it, lobby for it, protest for it, and march for it. Any suggestion that their free money might be cut off can trigger demonstrations and riots.

Politicians Want Votes

Politicians are *entrepreneurial* in this area of dispensing free money. Because they are eager to get the votes of these people who want more free money, they demand even more on their behalf. Of course, they mask their demands with dishonest appeals to "compassion" and "need," but the *real* reason, as opposed to the reason that *sounds good,* is that they hope to use these voters to get back into office at the next election.

If ever there is a suggestion that the flow of free money might be reduced or curtailed, cries of anguish and threats of disaster fill the air. But for some amazing reason, these potential tragedies never seem to occur. People, being expedient, always find a way to get by.

When Congress passed The Welfare Reform Act of 1996, hysterical politicians who had been riding on the backs of the poor into office year after year predicted widespread homelessness and a million starving children. Three years later, even the most skeptical observers had to admit that the level of homelessness had actually dropped, and that no child had missed a meal because of welfare reform.

After 1996, the employment rate of disadvantaged single mothers increased 50 percent to 100 percent. By 2004, there were 2.3 million fewer children in poverty than there were in 1996. The poverty rates of both black children and children of single mothers have been cut by one-third and are now at the lowest point in U.S. history.

Twisted Thinking

Recipients of free money soon develop elaborate excuses and justifications for why they are entitled to it. They claim that they are unfortunate, that they are *victims*, that they have been short-changed by society. "Society" owes them this money as compensation for what society has done to them or not done for them.

Simultaneously, the recipients of free money attack and demonize not only the sources of their free money—working people paying taxes—but anyone who questions the appropriateness of giving them even more. They are called "mean" or "stingy" or the favorite epithet of all, "racist."

Free money is destructive. Once a person begins to receive it on a regular basis, his self-respect, self-esteem, dignity, and self-reliance go down the drain. He becomes weak and grasping. He loses all sense of personal pride and independence.

People addicted to welfare and entitlements soon become desperate to hold onto them. As we said before, the fear of loss or "withdrawal" generates two and a half times the negative emotions of fear and anger as the idea of getting the money in the first place. The fastest way to get people into the streets demonstrating is to tell them that "those people are going to cut back or eliminate your free money." The scariest thing you can say to a senior citizen to get them to vote for you is that "those other people are going to take away your Social Security income."

People who are living off the sweat of others and who know in their hearts they make no contribution to the society they live in, soon become angry, hostile, and mean-spirited. With too much time on their hands and no work to do, they soon become easy prey for alcohol, drugs, petty crime, and other destructive behaviors that are common in the inner cities.

Why Do They Hate the Poor?

Imagine that there was an evil person with incredible power who *hated* poor people. Imagine that this evil, demented person wanted to punish poor people in the worst way possible. What would he do?

Assume that he is *evil* beyond comprehension. He hates poor people so much that he wants to destroy them financially, mentally, and emotionally, not just in the short term, but for their entire lives if possible and into the next generations of their families. What would be his best strategy?

The answer is simple: install a massive entitlement and welfare system and get as many people addicted to it as possible. Poor people, people at the lower end of the income scale, tend to be the most susceptible to the blandishments of free money. They often find it irresistible. They cannot stop themselves from reaching for it whenever it is offered.

If you want to really *hurt* these people, you make their very existence dependent on nameless, faceless, and usually uncaring bureaucrats. Force them to line up, fill out forms, and bare their souls in order to get their applications for free money approved. In this way, you rob them of their pride and dignity, disgrace them before their family and friends, and make them feel useless and incompetent. Then, if you really hate them, you make their children dependent as well and even pass laws making it illegal for unmarried mothers to live with the fathers of their children.

Helping the Less Fortunate

Jesus said, "The poor you will have always with you." For most of human history, everyone was poor. Until the nineteenth century, the word "poverty" was seldom used. It was generally assumed that the great masses were poor and that only a few people at the top were well off.

With the advent of the Industrial Revolution and the rapid improvements in living standards from 1815 onward, people became financially self-sufficient and even wealthy at the fastest rate in all of human history. For the first time, the poor actually become noticeable in contrast to the growing affluence of the population at large. It was at this time, in the wealthier societies, that doing something about the poor became *affordable* for the first time in history.

There is within the heart of every normal person the desire to help those who are less fortunate. In every society and at every level of society, people are motivated to lend a helping hand to the people around them who need it. This is a universal human trait.

Three Common Sentiments

In his important book *The Theory of Moral Sentiments,* Adam Smith, later to write *The Wealth of Nations,* explained that the three primary motivations of the normal person are *prudence, justice, and benevolence.*

Prudence was defined as the act of providing for oneself and one's family in the very best way possible. *Justice* meant supporting a legal and social system that protected one's life and property from the criminal behaviors of others. Once the needs of prudence and justice have been satisfied, every person turns normally and naturally toward *benevolence*, toward helping those who are in need of help.

When some politicians beat their breasts and claim loudly that they "care about people" while their opponents do not, they are engaging in falsehood and deception at the lowest level. The fact is *everyone* cares about others, starting in the family and expanding outward into society. The only difference between people and parties is the question, *"What is the best way to help people, both in the short term and in the long term?"*

Real versus False Benevolence
People who think short term, with little concern for the *secondary* consequences of their actions, believe that the natural urges toward benevolence are best served by taking money away from people who have earned it and giving it immediately to people who need it at the moment, whether or not this robs them of their self-esteem and makes them dependent on government in the long term.

People who think long term, who think about the secondary consequences of their actions, believe that *the best welfare program is a good job.* They believe that the best citizen is a proud, independent, self-reliant person who is in control of his own life. People who think long term do everything possible to encourage a vibrant business system that creates jobs, growth, hope, and opportunity for more people.

Short-term thinkers, grasping for easy votes by offering *free money,* are continually at war with long term thinkers who believe that the creation and maintenance of a prosperous society is the best way to provide for the greatest number of people.

Helping the Poor

In the 1800s, hundreds of voluntary groups, motivated by the spirit of benevolence, came together to set up "poor societies." These associations were organized by individuals and churches, staffed by volunteers, to work with the poor and unfortunate in cities and towns across the country. Their goals were to help people in difficulty to get back on their feet and become active and productive members of society.

In return for this assistance, recipients of help from these voluntary associations were required to abstain from drinking, to reconcile with their families whenever possible, to get cleaned up, learn new skills if necessary, and get paying jobs. In exchange, the poor societies helped and supported them until they were back on their feet. They channeled the E-Factor in the most positive and productive way. As a result, the success rate with this system of self-help was phenomenal.

Today, the Mormon Church has a similar system for church members who have fallen on hard times. But it is not *charity*. Even if the needy person is in a hospital bed, he is expected to make phone calls, or address envelopes. His self-respect is kept intact. The goal of the Mormon Church is a *whole person*, back in society making a contribution, a difference, as soon as possible. And each recipient of help from the church understands that, at any time, he can be called upon to offer assistance to someone else. One hand continually washes the other and as a result, there are no permanent welfare cases within the Mormon religion.

Something for Nothing Arises

In *The Tragedy of American Compassion*, author Marvin Olasky describes the evolution of American charity. He showed that when the government began offering welfare benefits at the beginning of the twentieth century, the first thing it did was cut away and eventually eliminate any of the strings that had been attached by private charities to this help.

People being weak, propelled by the E-Factor, following the line of least resistance, seeking *something for nothing* whenever possible, soon abandoned private charities and moved onto public assistance.

Perverse Incentives

It became even worse over time. Bureaucrats and government workers in the growing welfare bureaucracy were rewarded and promoted on the basis of *numbers*. How many people could they get onto the welfare rolls, and how much could they spend on these people?

Being expedient, clever government officials and department heads, aided by opportunistic politicians, lobbied and agitated for ever more welfare programs and government assistance to be made available to ever larger groups, with fewer and fewer requirements or restrictions.

To keep up their numbers, one by one the social service bureaucrats passed regulations to hold on to their welfare recipients once they had them dependent on the public purse. According to welfare regulations, a single mother living on welfare was forbidden to marry or even spend the night with the father of her illegitimate child. Welfare departments created "welfare police" who skulk around at night, attempting to catch a father sneaking in to spend time with the mother of his child. If he was caught, they threatened to throw the woman off welfare.

If a welfare recipient attempted to get a job or supplement his or her income, welfare bureaucrats slashed the benefits he or she was receiving so dramatically that they were able to discourage any attempt to achieve self-sufficiency.

Welfare recipients were not allowed to acquire property if they wanted to continue receiving the full range of benefits. If they had any money or property, they had to get rid of it as quickly as possible or be cut off from their free money. The system became completely dysfunctional, wreaking harm and havoc on everybody who was involved in it.

The Job Creation Machine
People who head up the state and federal welfare bureaucracies are usually college-educated, middle-class people who are well paid. Many senior welfare bureaucrats earn more than $100,000 per year to preside over the administration of welfare programs. They work in nice offices, live in nice neighborhoods, and drive recent model automobiles. Most of them have never met a poor person.

It gets even worse. Very often both husbands and wives work within the welfare bureaucracy (as well as in other government departments). Jointly, they earn $150,000 to $200,000 per year or more and are officially classified as "rich," if you listen to certain politicians.

After thirty years in the bureaucracy, they can retire with fully vested pensions, often at the age of fifty. They then move sideways to the next department, start at a new job paying them what they were earning at their old job and build up a second pension plan. This is the "double-dipping" I described earlier and is extremely popular in government today.

These people have become members of the "new elite" and live better than many doctors, lawyers, entrepreneurs, and other hard-working, highly-educated professionals. They never deal face-to-face with welfare recipients. They are too well-paid and important for that.

What Every Bureaucrat Wants

All up and down the line in the welfare bureaucracy, the E-Factor is at work. At every level, the six P's—Pay, Promotion, Position, Power, Perks, and Pensions—are tied into ever higher levels of funding. This requires ever more recipients of welfare programs receiving ever-greater amounts for doing nothing.

Until the welfare reforms of 1996, which were bitterly opposed as "obscene" and "cruel," the system was out of control. Third and fourth generations of welfare families were too common. Many children had grown up, had children and grandchildren, and never held a job in their lives. The inner cities around them collapsed into crime, violence, drug dealing, and dysfunction.

Turning Off the Tap

Since 1996, welfare caseloads have dropped 50 percent. Most welfare recipients, when they realized that the free money was going to be cut off, went out and got jobs. Today, those former welfare recipients are proud, contributing members of society. They are happy and respected members of their communities. They have "broken the habit," and they feel proud of themselves and their accomplishments.

J. C. Watts, former congressman from Oklahoma, worked hard in Congress to bring about these welfare reforms. His opponents accused him of "lacking compassion" for wanting to cut back on welfare programs and get people back into the economy with real jobs.

He replied to his accusers, *The difference between you and I is that you define 'compassion' by how many people you can make dependent on government. I define 'compassion' by how many people we can make independent of government."*

Double Detriment

The welfare mentality, the entitlement mindset, the desire to get *something for nothing*, is destructive in two major ways. First of all, it destroys the self-esteem, self-respect, and personal dignity of the recipient.

Second, it undermines the qualities of responsibility, self-reliance, and fairness upon which America is built. If someone consumes without producing, someone else must be forced to *produce without consuming*. The money he earns for himself and his family must be taken away from him in the form of taxation on his income to give to people who have made no effort to earn the money at all. Ultimately, all taxes come out of the paychecks and pockets of the working person. There is no other source of money.

Being legally deprived of the money you have earned, to have it given to others who don't or won't work for it, makes a person feel cheated and angry. For this reason, each politician, before he recommends any expansion of the flow of free money to any group, must ask the question, *"What would happen if everyone did what I recommend for some?"*

What would happen if everyone decided to go on welfare? What would happen if everyone decided that the best way to get the things they wanted was to manipulate government to get *something for nothing*?

As soon as you take any welfare policy recommendation to the extreme, to the possibility of *everyone's* taking advantage of it, you see immediately that the existence of most government give-away schemes depends on the assumption that most people won't apply for them. But this is no basis for sound government policy.

Think about the Children

Parents in general *love* their children. If you love your children, you want the very best for them. You want them to grow up proud and happy, confident and competent, capable of making a good life for themselves as adults.

The fact is, whatever you want for your own children, you should want for all other children. You should never encourage or condone any action or behavior for the children of other people that you would not want to have become a part of your family and happen to your children.

Our duty as citizens is to uncover and uproot any scheme that destroys people's pride and dignity by getting them addicted to free money. Especially, it is our civic duty to assure the very best for all our children by not allowing any structure of incentives that undermines their hopes for the future.

Look for the Real Reason

Your job is to recognize that the "reason that sounds good" is always based on compassion and generosity. But the "real reason" that any politician advocates any *something for nothing*, free money policy is to buy votes with other people's money, either directly or indirectly, with little or no concern for the long-term consequences of these policies.

Politicians and political policies that are short-sighted and expedient lie at the root of most of our social and economic problems today and have been responsible for the decline and fall of every great civilization in human history.

"The greatest thing a man can do in this world is to make the most possible out of the stuff that has been given him. This is success, and there is no other."

— Orison Swett Marden

Chapter Eleven

A Time for Truth

*"Guard your integrity as a sacred thing; nothing is at last
sacred but the integrity of your own soul."*

— Ralph Waldo Emerson

Most of our social, economic, and political problems are rooted
in the desire to get *something for nothing*, multiplied in intensity by the twin emotions of *envy* and *resentment*.

Just as the lowest common denominators of human nature
are *greed* and *laziness*, the fastest and easiest way to justify an
attempt to get *something for nothing* is to proclaim that those
who have what you want do not deserve it, and you do.

The tragedy is that it is impossible to build a coherent and
healthy philosophy and worldview on *negative emotions*, especially the desire to take away from others what you have not
earned. As soon as people begin to allow themselves to be guided by the destructive emotions of envy and resentment, they
become incapable of honesty, integrity, and rational thought.

The Two Worldviews

There are two general ways of looking at the world. A person
can have a *benevolent* worldview or a *malevolent* worldview.

A person with a benevolent worldview looks at life and the

world honestly and realistically, recognizing that there are many problems and deficiencies, but in the main it is a good place and definitely preferable to the alternatives.

This type of person tends to be *optimistic* about the future, looking for the good in people and situations, focusing on solutions rather than problems, and is generally positive, constructive, and hopeful.

People who have a benevolent worldview create everything good and worthwhile in society. They are the movers and shakers, the leaders and guides, the excellent parents, the entrepreneurs, scientists, poets, and creators of all good things. They are the spirit of America.

Stinkin' Thinkin'

People with a *malevolent* worldview, on the other hand, are primarily negative and cynical in their outlooks. They look for the worst in people and situations. They are characterized by low self-esteem and self-worth. They don't like themselves, and as a result, they don't like many others.

They see problems everywhere. They see injustice, oppression, unfairness, and inequalities of income and status. No solution is ever enough. No situation is ever satisfactory. For these people, there is always something wrong.

The person with a negative worldview must always have an *enemy.* Someone always has to be to blame for every problem affecting anyone, anywhere. Someone must be identified and punished.

It requires effort, imagination, and discipline to remain positive during the inevitable ups and downs of daily life.

But it takes no effort at all to become angry and resentful, lashing out at those who seem to be happier and more successful than you or others whose situation you take *personally.* The tragedy is that the more a person gives in to anger or negativity of any kind, the easier and more automatic it becomes for him to become and stay angry.

Anger, envy, and resentment feed upon each other until they consume the person who harbors them.They are totally destructive emotions and lie at the root of many of our problems in society today. It is said that *"anger is an acid that corrodes the vessel that contains it."*

Your Self-Esteem and Self-Image

The central role of self-esteem and self-image, how much you *like yourself* and how you *see yourself*, cannot be overemphasized.They constitute the person you are inside. These core elements of your personality have overwhelming affects on your worldview.

Each person has a deep inner need to feel important and valuable and be respected by others. Each person needs to believe in something bigger than himself. As Victor Frankl, founder of Logotherapy and author of *Man's Search for Meaning,* said, *"The deepest need of human beings is for a sense of meaning and purpose in life."*

However, America is a *meritocracy*, the first genuine meritocracy established in history. In a meritocracy, you are inevitably rewarded for your own personal merit and the value of the contribution you make to others.

But because people are driven by the E-Factor, by the tendency to be l*azy, greedy, selfish, ambitious, vain, ignorant, and impatient,* many seek rewards and results without effort or contribution.This is exactly the opposite of effective behavior in a meritocracy.

Political Opportunism
At the political level, there will always be opportunistic people who will offer to represent those who do not want to work for what they get. These opportunistic politicians will create elaborate arguments to prove why these prospective voters should be given free money.

As soon as the specter of free money, of *something for nothing* or very little, raises its ugly head, more and more people will attempt to get it.

The decline and fall of the Roman Empire came about when the Romans lost their drive to colonize and increase the wealth of their people. The leaders instead began offering the increasingly demanding populace "bread and circuses" to distract them, quiet them, and buy their votes and support, at least temporarily.

The welfare state of ancient Rome destroyed the empire from within, like a cancer, before the barbarians destroyed it with armed power from without.

The Test for Truth
The two great questions you have to ponder when considering any personal and government action are these: First, *"Is it true for me?"* Is what you are saying or hearing true for you, or do you think it may be true for others but not for yourself?
Listen to your inner voice. Be perfectly honest with yourself. Trust your own instincts. Only accept the premise or promise that feels right and is consistent with your own personal knowledge and experience.

Many of our most complex problems could be quickly resolved if each person were to ask themselves this question, *"Is this true for me?"* when considering the arguments and claims of politicians and activists who are driven by the E-Factor to achieve their goals the fastest and easiest way possible.

The second question you should ask is, *"What would happen if everyone did it?"*

Many ideas for free money and *something for nothing* quickly fall apart when they are held up against the possibility of everyone's engaging in a suggested behavior. They would be completely impossible.

Our Society Torn Apart

Let us examine some of the most emotionally divisive issues in our society today and see how they can be better understood in the light of the E-Factor, the desire to get *something for nothing* and the natural tendency to follow the path of least resistance to acquire money and power and the *safety, security, comfort, leisure, love, respect, and fulfillment* that go with them.

1. Affirmative Action and Welfare

There are two ways to get the material rewards you desire in our society. You can earn them yourself through hard work, or you can find some way to get the government to force someone to give them to you. Here is a simple question: *"Which is the easiest?"*

The questions surrounding race are complex and emotional. There was slavery, injustice, prejudice, and oppression for much of American history. They still exist through much of the world today.

In the 1960s, most of the legal barriers to full participation and equality were swept aside. Affirmative action laws were passed to help African Americans catch up.

The War on Poverty began under President Lyndon Johnson in 1964 with the unproven (and now disproven) idea that by giving people free money, they would soon become proud, productive members of society. Affirmative action was designed achieve this but be both remedial and temporary. It failed disastrously, primarily because it tried to contradict the E-Factor. It tried to make water flow uphill.

Moving Backward

From 1940 to 1960, according to African American economist Thomas Sowell, before the civil rights movement, the poverty rate among black families dropped from 87 percent to 47 percent. The relative incomes of blacks in comparison to whites *doubled* between 1936 and 1959. Rates of teenage pregnancy and venereal disease declined year after year. By every measure, black Americans were moving upward in almost every area. Then in the 1960s came affirmative action and the War on Poverty.

Thomas Sowell has written, *"The black family, which had endured centuries of slavery and discrimination, began rapidly disintegrating in the liberal welfare state that changed welfare from an emergency program to a way of life."*

Teenage pregnancies and illegitimate births increased to 65 percent of all black births. Violent crime, most of it black-on-black, soared. Urban riots increased. Welfare rates went through the roof. The *something for nothing* virus swept through the black community, destroying the hopes and dreams of a generation.

The Quota System

Affirmative action and the quotas for hiring and advancement that flow from it today quickly became barely disguised attempts to confer *something for nothing* on special groups. If companies are forced by law and threat of prosecution from the Equal Employment Opportunity Commission to hire unqualified minorities in proportion to their percentage of the local population, they will do it to avoid legal problems. But this short-term expedience does not develop talent, skill, or character in the beneficiary. It only serves to reinforce his perception of victimhood.

The cruelest thing you can do to any person, especially a member of a minority, is stigmatize him as "inferior" for life by using the power of government to put him in a position he has not earned and for which he is not qualified. Even if he has worked hard and is fully qualified for the position, because of affirmative action, he and others around him will always suspect he was not good enough to get the job on his own merits.

In higher education, there is ample evidence that affirmative action has hurt a large number of minority students who are admitted to universities for which they are not academically qualified. Because of the intense competition at these universities, they fare poorly, score lower grades, fall behind, and drop out at much higher rates than minority students who attend colleges with other students at their same grade level.

The fact is little racial prejudice remains in America today. The word *prejudice* means to "pre-judge." It means to form an opinion or make an assessment of a person in advance based on preconceived ideas or generalities not based on fact or experience. On this basis, most Americans are open, accepting, and non-judgmental of others before they get to know them and experience them firsthand.

In fact, there is probably more "reverse" prejudice than anything else. More Americans are willing to make special efforts to open up doors and create opportunities for minorities than ever before. No laws mandating this behavior are necessary. People do it out of a genuine feeling of benevolence for their fellow man or woman. No quotas or affirmative action are necessary.

Competition Brings Out the Best

In a free market society like the U.S., there is a continuous competition for talent and skill. Every business knows that the critical constraint on its ability to grow is competent people who can get results. Like cream rising to the top, people who can do a good job are hired sooner, paid more, and promoted faster. People who are not competent or motivated are not. No laws can change this. They can only mask it temporarily.

Some of the most talented and respected people in sports, business, show business, and public life are from minority groups. They are admired, esteemed, and successful for no other reason than because they are talented and do what they do in an excellent fashion. Think about people like Oprah, Tiger Woods, Bill Cosby, Michael Jordan, Morgan Freeman, and Denzel Washington.

In America, no one really cares about your background. In a meritocracy, all people really care about is your competence and your character right now. And this is under your control.

Compassion or Condescension

Compassion can quickly become *condescension*. Minority groups can become victims of what President George Bush called *"the soft bigotry of reduced expectations."* People begin to judge them by lower standards and expect less of them in comparison with others. This is completely unacceptable in America.

The way you bring the best out of people is by *challenging* them, by setting high standards, by demanding their "best game." You help people by encouraging them to aspire to excellence and treating them as if they have the potential to do more and be better than they ever have before.

The way you help people is by controlling the structure of

incentives, the "B" of the performance formula, and by not allowing them any other way to achieve their goals except by doing their best consistently and dependably.

2. Knowledge and Education

Knowledge and skill are the keys to opening the doors of opportunity in the twenty-first century. The more you learn and the better you get, the more opportunities you will have, the more you will be paid, and the faster you will be promoted. In a free society, in the absence of government interference and coercion, there is no other way.

The purpose of early education is to prepare young people to enter the workforce as adults and become valuable, proud, productive members of society. It is to enable young people to be free, independent, and capable of making a good living.

A System Gone Astray

The U.S. education system, once the best in the world (and still the best at the university level), has become a tragedy and a trap for most young people caught in it and unable to escape.

In 1947, 97 percent of Americans were literate, reading several books each year, and often each month. By 2004, fully 47 percent of Americans could not read above the seventh grade level. People who have not mastered the three R's by the time they leave school are destined to lifetimes of low income, underachievement, and wasted potential.

In the watershed study by the National Committee on Excellence in Education in 1983, "A Nation at Risk," several governors of American states concluded that our educational system was in such bad shape that *"if a foreign nation had done to America what our education system is doing to our young people, it would be considered an act of war."* If anything, the situation has gotten progressively worse over the years, especially for the most disadvantaged of our youth.

Today, African American students test at four grade levels below white and Asian students in the same schools. Even worse, they are not allowed to escape their failing schools, especially in the inner cities. They are trapped into lifetimes of below-average incomes, insecurity, and eventually envy, resentment, and feelings of victimhood.

Enter the Unions
The unleashing of the dogs of the E-Factor began when the first teachers union was formed in the 1950s. In a few years, driven by expediency, the focus of teaching shifted from student achievement to teacher pay and benefits. As Albert Schanker, head of the American Teachers Federation, once said, *"When the children start paying union dues, then we'll start caring about the children."*

Because of the structure of incentives in teaching, there is little motivation or reward for teaching or *not* teaching, much less teaching *well*. Once a teacher has tenure, he or she becomes almost impossible to discipline or fire. Teachers are paid solely on the basis of seniority, not quality. They receive the same pay whether they do a good job of teaching or not.

Even after countless studies showing that there is no relation between class size and student achievement, the teachers unions repeatedly called for more money for schools, higher pay for themselves, less work, smaller class sizes, and no performance standards at any time at any level. The national resistance to the 2001 bipartisan act, *No Child Left Behind*, by the teachers unions is a continuation of this resistance to standards of any kind.

The Teachers Unions and Politics

The teachers unions, representing most of the teachers in America, provide millions of dollars and thousands hours of labor to elect politicians who promise to block any attempt at educational reform. Because of their numbers, they have become one of the most powerful forces in modern politics.

The ultimate measure in the real world is *results*, but not in education. The end game in the teaching world is to process the students, educated or not, from one grade to the next, until they finally leave school.

Teachers are some of the highest paid non-professionals in America, often earning $50,000, $60,000, and even $70,000 for a nine-month year that is crammed with days off, vacations, and "Teachers' Conferences."

Competition Is the Key

The Economist magazine wrote on June 11, 2005, "The schools the poorest Americans attend have been getting worse rather than better. This is partly a problem of resources, to be sure. But it is even more a problem of bad ideas. The American educational establishment's weakness for airy-fairy notions about the evils of standards and competition is particularly damaging to poor children who have few educational resources of their own to fall back on. One poll of 900 professors of education, for example, found that 64 percent of them thought that schools should avoid competition."

The only way to reverse the pernicious effects of the E-Factor in education is to change the structure of incentives in such a way that academic excellence is pursued and rewarded. Without competition, there is no motivation to improve. Without competition, all the worst expressions of the E-Factor are encouraged.

Let the Parents Choose

The most important and impactful policy change in education would be *school choice*, allowing students and parents to choose their schools rather than being forced to stay in a school where the child is not learning. In the pursuit of academic excellence, Milton Friedman, Noble Prize-winning economist, first proposed school choice and the "voucher system" in the 1960s. The idea is simple. The United States spends an average of about $9,000 per student per year in the K-12 system, almost equivalent to private school tuition. With a voucher system, each parent would receive a voucher for each child of school age that could be "spent" at any school—public, private, or parochial— that the parent chose. The money would follow the student, not just go automatically to the school.

Against extraordinary opposition by the teachers unions, this system was introduced by African American legislator Polly Williams and Wisconsin governor Tommy Thompson to the Milwaukee School System some years ago. It was so successful in increasing competition and school grades that it spread to more schools and additional states. In 2002, the Supreme Court decided that school choice was legal under the Constitution. In 2005, Cleveland expanded its school choice program and approved 14,000 more vouchers to enable students to escape from failing schools.

In addition to vouchers and school choice, principals must be allowed to fire poor teachers (not possible today) and make everyone accountable. Without competition and standards, education in public schools deteriorates, leaving entire generations of poor students unable to read, write, and participate in the American Dream as adults.

The fact is, no matter how pleasant they appear on the outside, teachers, like everyone else, are *lazy, greedy, selfish, ambitious, vain, ignorant, and impatient.* They all want *safety, security (job), comfort, leisure, love, respect, and fulfillment.* To achieve these ends, they strive for more power and money, and no amount is ever enough.

The 80/20 Rule in Education

It is generally assumed in public education that the 80/20 Rule applies. Twenty percent of the students will do well no matter how good or bad the teaching or the school; 80 percent will do poorly. This is why they say *"the private schools produce the leaders and managers while the public schools produce the workers."* Nationwide, 21.5 percent of public school teachers have their children in private schools. This is outrageous!

The only cure for the educational system, the only way to assure that every child gets an education that prepares them to be able to realize the American Dream, is to introduce competition for academic excellence at all levels of the school system, both private and public.

Wherever competition has been tried, academic accomplishment and grade levels increase immediately. Wherever there is no competition, children are educationally short-changed. They never reach their full potential. They are put out into the workforce without the ability to provide for themselves and create the kind of lives they desire for themselves and their families.

3. Immigration—Legal and Illegal

Immigration can be either a blessing or a curse, depending on *three* things: first, is it legal or illegal? The United States accepts more than one million legal immigrants each year, more than all other countries in the world put together. If someone comes here legally, they have usually been carefully vetted through the proper political process and are much more likely to become valuable, contributing members of American society.

If the immigrant is *illegal*, this means that the first act of this person in coming to America is to break the law. If his or her first American experience is that of law-breaking, and getting away with it, the seeds are sown for further law-breaking later on. This is why our prisons are jammed with thousands of illegal immigrants who have committed crimes against people and property, including mass murder. They arrived as criminals and then continued their lives of crime.

Second, is the immigrant qualified and skilled or unqualified and unskilled? If the immigrant is capable of making a valuable contribution to society by participating in the process of producing goods and services that customers want, he can make a good life for himself while being a benefit to his community. If the immigrant is uneducated and unskilled, his ability to become a valuable member of society is diminished, if not eliminated entirely, at least in the short term.

Third, is the motivation for immigration positive or negative?

Does the new immigrant come seeking *opportunity*, or does he come to America seeking welfare and handouts? Does he or she look for a job or for ways to *game the system* for benefits, welfare, free medical care, and free education?

The E-Factor and Immigration

The E-Factor is evident early in the immigration process. In Mexico, they sell information kits to prospective illegal immigrants instructing them on how to get false documents once they get into America. They learn how to use those documents to apply for welfare, unemployment benefits, disability payments, and free services, all of which are to be paid by taxpayers.

Opportunistic politicians encourage and promote illegal immigration by passing laws making it illegal for hospitals or schools to require proof of citizenship before providing services. This ability to escape detection in the use of public services is widely known throughout Latin America and other countries. It creates tremendous incentives for expedient behavior among potential illegal immigrants.

Shutting the Door
Expedient politicians lobby for bilingual education, even though they know that it has been proven to be completely *ineffective*. A child forced into bilingual education emerges after a certain time *illiterate* in both languages, usually Spanish and English.

Lack of English literacy slams the door in the face of even the most sincere, aspiring young person. Over time, bilingual education and lowered teaching standards in inner-city schools create an uneducated, resentful, lower class who are blocked from achieving the American Dream, but whose votes and support can be manipulated by clever politicians. In most cases, these politicians know *exactly* what they are doing and what social situation they are creating for the future. After all, they are expedient.

They then use demagogic techniques to fan the flames of envy and resentment. They encourage illegal and illiterate immigrants to blame all their problems on tax-paying citizens who complain about being taxed and penalized to provide them with free money, education, and medical services. People who think it is unfair, unjust, and wrong to be forced to provide for illegal immigrants who have broken the law to enter this country are demonized as "lacking compassion" or being "racist."

Enforce the Law

The solution for illegal immigration is to simply enforce the laws against it, to make it expedient *not* to enter the country illegally by severely punishing anyone who does.

There are officially seven million *illegal* immigrants in America today. Unofficially, the estimate is as high as three times that number, as many as twenty-one million people, spread out all over the country.

In the absence of political will and courage to enforce our laws, the U.S. is putting its future as a dynamic country with a common language and heritage at risk. By continually making it attractive for people to come to the United States illegally, we are creating social and political problems that will take generations to solve.

4. Lawyers and Lawsuits

The outgoing president of the American Bar Association, addressing a national convention of lawyers, asked the following question, *"What is the difference between a lawyer and a catfish?"*

After a few moments, he gave the answer. *"One is a garbage eating, scum-sucking, bottom dweller. The other is just a fish."*

The heroes and heroines in the legal profession today, the ones who receive grand accolades and standing ovations, are those who have demonstrated the ability to extract massive damage settlements out of gullible juries for questionable offenses.

The Lawsuit Industry

Lawyers and lawsuits are tearing America apart, pitting everyone against everyone else in the legal lottery called "sue thy neighbor." They are another example of the E-Factor and the obsession with getting *something for nothing* gone crazy.

Tort lawyers today, hiding behind the law, have become some of the most immoral, unethical, and uncaring people in our society. Aided and abetted by judges to whose elections campaigns they contribute, and craven politicians, most of whom are paid off by the trial lawyers in the form of "campaign contributions," these lawyers are wreaking chaos and destruction everywhere.

As soon as the door opened to "contingency fees," where lawyers, like hucksters, carnival barkers, and used car salesman, work on *commission*, the flood of frivolous lawsuits began. Today, it is out of control. Only 16 percent of Americans, according to the Wall Street Journal, feel the legal system can protect them against frivolous and potentially ruinous lawsuits.

Only in America

In all other countries and in the U.S. until the 1960s, the legal rule was, "loser pays." If you filed a lawsuit and lost, you were required to pay the costs of the defense of the other party, plus all other legal expenses.

In the 1960s, clever lawyers and compliant judges eliminated this rule. Today, anyone can sue anyone else for anything, no matter what the basis. If you are sued, you must either hire a lawyer and defend yourself, usually at great cost, or lose the judgment by default. Since it is fairly easy to find a lawyer who will bring a lawsuit against you on "contingency," and impossible to find a lawyer who will defend you without advance payment, you can spend a fortune defending yourself against a completely frivolous claim, while the person suing you pays nothing.

Tort lawyers claim to be concerned about getting "justice for the little guy." They loudly proclaim that their only concern is to represent injured people who, except for contingency fees, could not otherwise afford to hire them. In reality, these lawyers are examples of the E-Factor run amok.

They are often smooth-talking, slick operators who easily mislead both complainants and defendants into believing that they care about "justice" and righting wrongs. They purport to be working for the *powerless* against the *powerful*.

In reality, they are more often rapacious, greedy professionals driven mad by the smell of "free money," just as piranhas in the Amazon are driven wild by the smell of blood. Many of them make millions of dollars each year in "extortion-like lawsuits," and a few of them have even become billionaires.

The Worst Get on Top

The most successful tort lawyers are the worst and the most unethical of all. They have developed the ability to smell out cases where they can emotionally manipulate a jury into granting huge damages for questionable offenses or no offenses at all. Vice presidential candidate John Edwards, whose father was a mill worker, is reportedly worth seventy million dollars today, most of it earned suing doctors and hospitals for not having performed enough Caesarean births, thereby supposedly causing the child to be born with cerebral palsy. Exhaustive medical research has proven that there is *zero* relationship between the number of Caesarean births and cerebral palsy in children. Instead, it is an undetectable and incurable genetic defect. Nonetheless, John Edwards is rich today and many doctors' careers have been destroyed.

Working the System

These lawyers are extraordinarily skilled at "jury selection," identifying compliant jurors they know they can manipulate easily. They contribute heavily to the candidacies of judges who they will soon appear before arguing their cases. They use a network of "junk scientists," pseudo-experts who move from court to court to testify again and again on the basis of questionable science or data. One radiologist profiled recently had reviewed 32,000 x-rays sent to him by tort lawyers and found that all 32,000 had asbestos-related scarring.

Recently, an objective panel of radiologists carefully scrutinized the x-rays of several hundred people who had sued for asbestos-related injuries. Whereas the junk science doctors who had testified for the complainants had found asbestos-related scarring in 96 percent of the x-rays, the objective panel of radiologists found asbestos scarring in only 4 percent of the x-rays submitted for examination. Every year, countless millions of dollars are awarded to people based on this type of science.

Everyone Pays the Damages

The threats and costs of lawsuits have driven many doctors out of medicine and increased health-care costs for the average person by 25 percent to 50 percent. Because of the out-of-control tort lawsuits, brought against any doctor when any procedure is unsuccessful, more and more people are unable to get medical attention in certain states and parts of the country.

According to estimates, lawsuits and the threats of lawsuits cost the average family of four an additional $3200 per year in increased costs. This money has to be paid in higher prices for products of lower quality. It comes out of the pockets of the average working man and off of their tables. It is money they don't have to spend on their wives and children.

The only solution for an out-of-control legal system is clear legislation that brings back the "loser pays" principle and strictly limits legal liability. The entire structure of incentives in the tort industry must be upended. It must not be possible for clever lawyers, interested only in getting *something for nothing* or very little, to ply their evil wares.

5. Rolling the Dice

Gambling is perhaps the most perfect example of the desire to get *something for nothing.* The whole idea behind gambling is there is some fast, easy way to get money that you have not earned.

Proponents of legalized gambling declare that it is an innocent form of entertainment "fun for the whole family." But gamblers always lose *eventually.* It is only a matter of time. The billion-dollar casinos and gambling resorts have not been built with "losses."

According to economist Alan Meister in his new "Indian Gaming Industry Report," the nation's 405 Indian casinos generated about nineteen billion dollars in revenues last year, up from zero a few years ago. In other estimates, these tribes and casinos contributed more than $800 million in 2004 to various politicians, making them the biggest and most powerful political lobbying group in the world. Not surprisingly, most tribal casino revenues are almost impossible to verify. No one knows for sure how much is going to which people for what purposes.

Gambling Destroys the Gambler

The main objection to gambling is not that most people are losing money that could be better spent on their families. The worst aspect of the "gambling bug" is it destroys the gambler's capacity to deal with reality. According to psychologists, when gamblers win, they consider it to be a matter of personal skill. When they lose, however, they define the situation not as "losing" but as "almost winning." They create a fantasy world around gambling and attempt to live in it.

Gambling corrupts the soul and makes the gambler negative, distrustful, and angry. Continued losing undermines his self-esteem and destroys his self-respect.

For every gambling loss, there is an opponent, as in poker, or a dealer/croupier, as in black jack or roulette, who *wins*. The loser is always being defeated by someone visible and real. As a result, he ends up feeling frustrated and bitter. He *feels* like a loser.

The act of gambling opens up the mind to every other possibility of getting *something for nothing*, and like a syphilis spirochete, the gambling idea soon lodges in the brain, causing a form of insanity, destroying both the person and his or her family.

To Hell and Back

A reporter for National Review wrote recently, *"I have been to hell and returned. It is a place called Las Vegas in the Nevada desert."* He went on to write about the casinos filled with working men and women, grim-faced, betting and losing their rent money, money that could be better spent on their children. Anyone who has walked through a casino has noticed the strained faces and lack of joy among the people for whom the loss of their hard-earned money is only a matter of time.

It is not possible to outlaw gambling. But like an addictive narcotic, the only way you can avoid its destructive effects is to avoid it altogether. You can recognize that it is an attempt to get *something for nothing,* which is inherently wrong. Worse, it weakens your moral immune system and makes you susceptible to other temptations to get *something for nothing.*

6. Health, Energy, and Longevity

The desire to be fit, healthy, and live a long life is perhaps the most common of all of human desires and the basic need of all human beings. George Gilder said recently, *"Longevity is now the most precious of all commodities in our society."*

But where did people ever get the idea that medical attention was a *right*, guaranteed them by a benevolent government or employer, at little or no cost? The *something for nothing* virus runs rampant in all areas of healthcare today. People do things to their bodies that are virtually guaranteed to undermine their health and shorten their lives. They then demand the medical and pharmaceutical industry somehow take responsibility to return them to health and wholeness, at little or no cost to themselves.

The Formula for Health and Long Life

Everyone today knows the five-word formula for health and fitness: *"Eat less and exercise more."* It has never been otherwise. These five words summarize the best findings of hundreds of books and thousands of articles. The key is to practice them daily.

The epidemic of obesity, with 60 percent of Americans either overweight or seriously overweight, is a direct result of thinking that you can have *"health for nothing."*

Obesity numbers grow as more people become addicted to *something for nothing* in other areas of their lives. They soon begin to see themselves as *victims*. They resent others who are fit and trim. They lash out and blame either their "hormones" or the companies that sell them the food that they eat too much of.

HealthCare for Nothing

In a "third party payer" system of company health insurance and HMOs, most people consume medical services without knowing or caring how much they really cost. It doesn't matter to them as long as "someone else" is paying for it.

Medical attention is loudly trumpeted as a "right." But every right includes a *responsibility*. If you have the right to medical attention, this means someone else has the responsibility of providing it to you. Someone has to pay.

No one assumes a "right" to food, clothing, shelter, or transportation, even though these are basic necessities of life. These factors have to be earned and paid for according to your capacity.

Economists say, *"There is no demand curve for a free good."* What this means is, if something of value is free, the demand for that commodity soon becomes *unlimited*. People will consume as much of it as they possibly can without restraint.

The Canadian Experience

In Canada, which is often held up as a model of national health-care, medicine is supposedly "free." However, you know that nothing is really free. Everything has to be paid by someone, somehow. Medical care represents about 13 percent of the Canadian GNP and is inferior to U.S. medical care in every way.

In the U.S., by contrast, medical costs run at about 14 percent of GNP, but because these costs are largely determined in a free market, we have the best medical system in the world.

Anyone who has experienced both systems will attest to the *night and day* difference between them. This is why people come from Canada and all over the world to seek medical treatment in the U.S. But people in the U.S. seldom go to any other country.

In Canada, to stop runaway costs from bankrupting the government, medical care is carefully rationed. Hospitals are shut down to limit use. If you are over sixty, it becomes harder and harder to get treated for chronic illnesses. The waiting lists are endless, usually many months or even longer. Not only that, it is a crime, punishable by imprisonment in Canada, for either a doctor to *offer* treatment outside the national system or for a patient to *pay* for treatment not sanctioned by the government. Everyone must wait in the same line and get the same treatment by law.

However, this may be coming to an end. In 2005, the Quebec Supreme Court kicked the chair out from under the "free" Canadian health system by ruling that "access to a waiting list is not access to healthcare," as guaranteed by the Canadian Bill of Rights.

The Best Medical System

In the United States, because of competition and the free market, virtually anyone can get care for almost any need quickly and efficiently. Even a person with no health insurance, no address, and no visible means of support can go to the outpatient department of any hospital in America and get treatment for an accident or an emergency without charge. This is the law. The inescapable fact is each person is responsible for his or her own level of fitness, weight, and health. There is no *something for nothing* in health and longevity. Everything must be paid for by someone. Nothing is ultimately free.

The Healthcare Insurance "Crisis"

One of the problems of healthcare insurance today is that too many people look upon buying this insurance as a gamble, like shooting craps or playing black jack. Sometimes they win; sometimes they lose.

According to careful analysis, only about 3 percent of people without health insurance in America are in that situation *involuntarily.* Most people without health insurance have decided to gamble that they won't be sick or injured. They choose instead to spend the money on their lifestyles or other things. Many of these "uninsured" have annual incomes of $50,000 or more.

Just as there are people who avoid buying liability or accident insurance for their cars, gambling that they will not get into an accident, there are people who decline to insure themselves medically, hoping they will not need medical attention.

Health insurance is only another term for "prepaid medical expenses." Health insurance premiums are set based on accurate projections and estimates of what a person is likely to spend per year on health services. Health insurance premiums are simply monies that are pooled to pay for the inevitable and predictable healthcare costs when they come. It is not possible to get health for nothing, fitness for nothing, long life for nothing. The price of health and longevity must always be paid, sooner or later.

There Is Always a Solution
The solution to the so-called "healthcare crisis" in America is private health accounts where individuals pay for their own healthcare and insurance and keep the savings when they manage their health intelligently. The best solution of all would be to allow all Americans the incredibly wide range of choices and options for healthcare that all elected officials, even when retired, and all members of government unions receive at taxpayers' expense. Our healthcare problems would be over.

7. *The Families of America*

Parents and children are the fundamental unit of our society. In thinking about the long term, they are also the most important. The primary purpose of each generation is to bring up and provide for the next generation.

How a child is raised to adulthood not only impacts that child, but his or her spouse, their children, their children's children, and on into the third and fourth generations. Each of us is still affected as an adult by the way our grandparents treated our parents when they were growing up.

You Are Responsible

Government cannot raise children. It can only create an environment in which children can be brought up happy, healthy, and self-sufficient.

The responsibility for raising happy, healthy children lies with their parents. No child asks to be born. But once born, his parents are responsible for providing for him in every way, physically, mentally, and emotionally.

Many parents want to get something for nothing in child rearing. They want to be seen as excellent parents without paying the price that this requires.

How does a child spell "love"? Answer: "T-I-M-E!"

The value of each relationship in your life is determined by how much of your personal time that you invest in it. You can only increase the value and quality of a relationship by investing more minutes and hours in one-on-one, face-to-face, heart-to-heart communications with your spouse and children.

Something for nothing parents try to get by on the cheap, spending their precious and irreplaceable time in all the wrong places.

The solution to the problems of marriage and parenting is simple. Spend more time with the people you care about the most.

Happiness Is the Goal

Psychologists estimate that 85 percent of your happiness in life will come from relationships with others. Only 15 percent of life satisfaction comes from external results, rewards, and accomplishments. No one on his deathbed ever said, *"I wish I'd spent more time at the office."*

The key to self-esteem, self-respect, and personal pride is to place your important relationships in the center of your life, as the sun in your personal solar system, and organize all the other activities of your life to orbit around them.

8. Environmentalism and Activism

The desires to do good and to improve the lives of others, to "save the world," are the first fallback positions of a person seeking meaning and purpose in life. Virtually all forms of environmentalism and activism are clear illustrations of the *something for nothing* drive gone out of control.

Abigail Adams once wrote, *"All men would be tyrants if they could."* Nietzsche called it the "will to power." This applies to many women as well.

There is a dark streak deep in the soul of many people that drives them to want to command and control others. As Lord Acton wrote, *"Power corrupts and absolute power corrupts absolutely."* Even the thought of obtaining power over others corrupts the soul.

Looking for a Cause
Well-meaning people, seeking something bigger than themselves to believe in, often become interested in a cause of some kind that they feel is important to society, like saving the environment or the whales.

In too many cases, these people are unemployed or *unemployable*. They have time on their hands and few prospects. They seek something to which they can dedicate themselves.

They become what Eric Hoffer called the "true believers," going from cause to cause throughout their lives.

The first thing these people discover, much to their shock and amazement, is that many people are either indifferent to their worthy causes or completely hostile to their ideas.

The second thing they discover is that they need *money* if they are going to accomplish anything. Of course, they need money to underwrite their activities, but especially they need money to pay their personal bills.

Suddenly, the *something for nothing* bug bites them. They begin looking for ways to get money from others to pursue their activities, to further their causes.

Competition Appears

They then notice there are lots of other people trying to get money for other worthy causes in competition with them. To survive, they become more determined to make their case and win support. To compete with others, they are forced to make a better case, preferably loudly and publicly. They look around for politicians who think that by espousing a particular cause they can get more votes. They gather members to more effectively impress their potential political sponsors. As always happens, the worst people in these movements, the most clever and passionate, soon rise to the top and take over.

They open offices, hire people, begin lobbying, and looking for ever more *free money* to pay the bills. Hierarchies form within these organizations, salaries are paid, people start to make good money, often more than they have ever made before.

The single, most burning, intense desire of these people is to get the government to seize control of property and assets. They want to *force* people to do things that they would not do voluntarily but which activists feel they should be *made* to do.

Saving the World

In the case of environmentalists for example, they want control and power for *nothing*. They want to control land or property they don't own and won't buy.

To whip up more support, they blame the situation that they feel requires mending on someone, somewhere. Once they have decided on a *villain*, an enemy, usually someone who owns a business or property, they pull out all stops to demonize him and get control of his assets.

For example, a few years ago, an environmental group needing money made up the "Alar Scare." The entire nation was subjected to televised hearings, listening to actress Meryl Streep and others creating a panic, decrying the danger of Alar in apples.

By the time this "junk science" had been refuted, and it was proven that no one had ever been harmed by Alar, which had been used as a preservative for fifty years, the damage was done. Hundreds of apple growers had their crops destroyed, and many of them went bankrupt.

When the dust finally settled, the environmental group that had orchestrated the national panic admitted that they needed a big scare to raise funds to keep their organization going. Jobs and paychecks, *something for nothing,* were at stake.

Free Money Keeps Them Going

The drive behind most activism is *something for nothing* as well. These organizations need money to pay salaries and expenses. The only source of this unearned money is individual or corporate donors and, of course, the government. Their "product" is the ability to activate public opinion and scare opportunistic politicians with their numbers.

In return, these environmentalists and activists get money and power they have not earned and do not deserve. They create jobs for themselves with paychecks, expense accounts, and junkets to conferences where they often travel in limousines and stay in beautiful hotels. They often spend most of the money they raise on "expenses," with very little actually going to the "worthy cause."

Thieves in Sheep's Clothing

The only solution to environmentalism and activism out of control is to expose them for what they are: thieves posing as concerned citizens, supposedly motivated by compassion but actually obsessed with dispossessing others of their money and property.

You can tell if these people are "sincere" in their convictions by a simple test. *How much of their own money have they personally invested in furthering their cause?* In most cases, they have no money of their own at all. They are poor and looking to activism as a way to create jobs for themselves and their friends.

In some cases, they do have money, but they very seldom spend any of their own money on causes they believe other people should contribute to. All they want is *something for nothing,* but coming to them, not from them.

What Is to Be Done?

In every area of human life and activity, the E-Factor reigns supreme. Like gravity, it is to be assumed in advance as the basic operating principle of all human behavior. The onus of proof must be on the person who denies that he is acting expediently to prove that he is not *lazy, greedy, ambitious, selfish, vain, ignorant, and impatient.* This turns out to be almost impossible to do.

Each person in each position in any organization, especially

political organizations, where there are no measurable performance standards, is *lazy, greedy, selfish, ambitious, vain, ignorant, and impatient.* He strives for money and power to get the
safety, security, comfort, leisure, love, respect, and fulfillment
he desires.

The only variable, the only modifying influence in the ABC
Formula of human performance is the *structure of incentives.*
The only difference between people is how they choose to go
about accomplishing their common ends.

Think about the Long Term

Men and women of *character* think long term. They think about
the secondary consequences of their behaviors. They strive to
get the things they want through voluntary cooperation. They
practice honesty, integrity, and openness with others. The results
of their behaviors turn out to be beneficial for everyone
involved, both in the short term and in the long term.

Further down the scale of human character, too many people,
behaving expediently, engage in dishonest and corrupt behaviors to get the things they want the fastest and easiest way possible. They are not concerned about the long-term effects of
their actions.

Return to Values

The way to solve any human problem is by a return to *values.* It
is first of all to clarify exactly the values that the organization or
individual stands for and then to organize all the activities of the
individual or organization so that they behave consistent with
those values, no matter what the short-term temptation might
be. Only in this way can the irresistible power of the E-Factor be
banked, channeled, and directed toward positive outcomes that
benefit everyone involved.

Something for Nothing

"No matter what we want out of life, we have to give up something to get it."

—Raymond Holliwell

Chapter Twelve

America and the World

"People, when they first come to America, whether as travelers or settlers, become aware of a new, agreeable feeling; that the whole country is their oyster."

— Alistair Cooke

America is a great country, easily the best country in all of human history, on any measure you care to use. As it happens, citizens of every country feel that their own country is superior in some way to all others, whether or not this idea is based on fact. But in the case of the United States, it is true.

"American exceptionalism" is well founded, rooted in the ideas of the American Revolution. Americans are an exceptional people in many measurable and quantifiable ways.

Does this mean that Americans are *superior?* Of course not. America is a melting pot made up of people from every nation in the world. However, Americans who embrace the American ideals are exceptional on the basis of provable and objective measures.

The Good Life

As I mentioned earlier, there are four elements of the good life that people the world over have sought throughout history. These are the core ingredients that make for happiness as a human being. Each country can be graded on a scale measuring how many of these key goals are achievable, by how many people, and how long the average person has to work to achieve them.

Living a Long Life

The first element of a good life consists of *health, energy, and longevity.* American medicine at all levels is the finest in the world. Individuals from any economic group can live longer and better in America than has ever been possible before. One of the fastest growing age groups in the United States is the population over one hundred years old. No one ever leaves America to seek medical attention in other countries. But anyone who can afford the cost comes to America when they cannot get the medical attention they need in their home country.

Having a Happy Family

The second ingredient of the good life is a *happy, healthy family,* characterized by high-quality human relationships at home and in one's community. More than any other measure, the ability of individuals and their families to achieve the basic human goals of *safety, security, comfort, leisure, love, respect, and fulfillment* is more possible for people living in America than for the residents of any other country.

Doing a Great Job

The third ingredient of the good life is *meaningful, well-paid work* that one enjoys and one feels makes a difference in society. The United States has the most flexible, wide-open labor market in the world, where anyone from anywhere can come and rise as high and as fast as he desires solely based on his own effort and his own willingness to make a valuable contribution to the lives and work of others. American workers enjoy the highest standards of living of any people in the world and have more than 100,000 different jobs to choose from.

Achieving Financial Independence

The final ingredient, the icing on the cake that constitutes the good life, is the achievement of *financial independence*. Perhaps the greatest fear that people have is the fear of poverty, of being broke or destitute, especially in old age. In the United States, it is more possible for more people, in more different ways, to achieve financial independence and provide for their retirement than in perhaps any other country. Today, our senior citizens are the most affluent of any senior group in history.

How Can You Measure a Country?

The secretary of Education, Bill Bennett, was one asked by a high school student, "How can you tell if the United States is a good country or not?"

He replied, "That's simple; just use the 'Gate Test.'"

"What is the Gate Test?" asked the student.

"Well," replied Secretary Bennett, "Just raise the gates and watch which way the people go."

People from 194 countries have flocked to the United States for more than 200 years, arriving both legally (one million per year) and illegally (21 million as of 2004).

These people have surged through the open gates to participate in the American Dream of hope and opportunity. One of the main jobs of the United States in the world is to remain the guardian of the "American Dream."

The American Dream

There is no other country in the world or in history that has had the word "Dream" attached to it. There is no "German Dream" or "French Dream" or "Russian Dream." There is only the "American Dream."

In his 1986 State of the Union speech, President Ronald Reagan, addressing the Joint Session of Congress, said, *"America is the first country in the world where nobody cares who your parents were."*

He said, *"You can move to Paris and live there all your life and never be accepted as French. You can move to London and live there all your life and never be accepted as British. You can move to Berlin and live all your life and never be accepted as German. But you can move to America and be accepted as an American from the first day."*

The American Spirit

There is another reason for the well-founded notion of "American Exceptionalism." There are dozens of admirable human qualities, but the seven great virtues are probably those of *Integrity, Courage, Industriousness, Generosity, Sincerity, Responsibility, and Persistence.* These qualities may be possessed by individuals from every nationality, to one degree or another. But there is no country on earth where these qualities are more encouraged and rewarded than in the United States.

There is something in the philosophic, democratic, spiritual, emotional, and idealistic climate of the United States that conspires to bring out the highest and best of these qualities in the greatest number of people. These qualities form the foundation for the entrepreneurial boldness and energy that has made the United States the innovative industrial and technological powerhouse of the world for more than one hundred years.

The Economic Powerhouse

America, starting off as an unexplored continent 400 years ago, produces more goods and services than all twenty-five countries of Europe together, even though many of them go back 2000 years or more. America shares her wealth by giving more in foreign aid, public and private, each year, than all the other countries in the world put together.

America is a great country because its people in the main, are *idealistic, generous, entrepreneurial, hard-working, visionary, and courageous.* These qualities are held in higher esteem in America than they are in any other country, where they are often under continuous attack.

An article in a French newspaper recently, decrying the booming free market economy of America, characterized by high levels of entrepreneurial activity and continuous job-changing, contained these words, *"We have no interest in the American economic system. We French prefer a tightly regulated and highly controlled way of life. After all, America is made up of the people who left. France is made up of the people who stayed."*

Born Out of Revolution

Americans fought for the ideals of *freedom, liberty, individualism, personal responsibility, and limited government* in the Revolutionary War and have labored and fought for them ever since. This can be said of no other country.

The American Declaration of Independence, the Constitution, and the Bill of Rights are thought by many to be divinely inspired. The United States was designed from the beginning to be the "last best hope of mankind," a place where anyone could come and create a better life. America was the first country set up to be supportive of the best interests of the "little guy."

Freedom and Free Enterprise

President Calvin Coolidge once said, *"The business of America is business."*

By this he meant that the business of America is to protect, preserve, and promote the capitalist system of free enterprise. This is the greatest system ever discovered and developed to create hope, opportunity, and wealth for the greatest number of people. Americans working together in peaceful cooperation, within a framework of law and order, have created a system that pours out an almost unimaginable cornucopia of products and services to improve the lives and work of the average person.

It is our system and the remarkable melting pot of Americans who thrive within it that have made America the wealthiest and most powerful country in the world. Our national spirit, not our natural resources, is the basis of American exceptionalism. It makes the United States different and superior to all other countries.

Foreign Policy

After being defeated in World War II, Germany was divided into four zones of occupation—the American, British, French, and Russian. It was generally believed at that time that there was a militaristic impulse within the German people that caused them to make war on their neighbors. The country was broken up so that this could not happen again, as it had just happened in World War I and World War II.

However, detailed work by historians in the next few years found that Germany was no more or no less of a warmongering nation than many other countries. In fact, in European history, it turned out Sweden had initiated more wars of conquest than any other nation, followed closely by France. Germany was third. The question then became, *"What is it that causes a nation to go to war?"*

The discovered answer was insightful and revealing. Historians concluded that whenever a nation reached a critical size or level of power relative to its neighbors and felt that it could attack another nation and win, that nation became an aggressor and went to war.

Aggression with Impunity

The only factor that stopped nations from going to war throughout history was the conclusion of the leaders that they could not succeed. If they went to war, they would be worse off as a result. The price was too high.

To forestall this natural warlike tendency, nations entered into alliances with other nations to maintain balances of power against potentially aggressive countries. These balances of power shifted continually as nations rose and fell in terms of their military capability. But throughout history, every nation, if it grew powerful enough in its own estimate, would become an aggressor and attack whatever nation or nations it considered weaker and vulnerable to conquest.

In other words, the thought of getting *something for nothing* in conquering another country turned out to be the primary motivator of war, militarism, and imperialism throughout history.

Looting and Plundering

The French Revolution was supposedly based on "Liberty, Equality, and Fraternity," noble ideals for mankind. But when French forces, under Napoleon, attacked and dominated all of Europe in every direction the very first action of French troops upon conquering a city or country was to loot and plunder, sending cartloads and shiploads of gold, silver, jewels, and artwork back to Paris.

The very first of act of the Nazis when they overran Europe from1939-1945 was to loot and plunder the banks, treasuries, and art collections of the conquered lands. When Russia pushed the Nazis back in Eastern Europe, the very first act of Russian occupying forces was to loot and plunder whatever was left.

When the Japanese invaded Manchuria in 1938, and then China, "loot and plunder" was at the top of the list. When they went on to invade Hong Kong, the Philippines, Indochina, Malaysia, and Singapore, looting took precedence over all other activities. Regardless of all claims of national purpose or high philosophy, the primary reason for initiating aggressive wars has always been to loot and plunder, to attempt to get *something for nothing*, as much and for as long as possible.

The American Exception
Historians who carried out this study came to a remarkable conclusion. They found, alone amongst all the nations of history, America was the only country that had reached "critical mass," with the size and power necessary to overrun other countries, and refused to become an imperial power. In simple terms, as far as the United States was concerned, *"The business of America is business."*

There was and still exists a deep strain of *isolationism* in the American character. Protected on both sides by huge oceans, the United States just wants to be left alone to carry on and conduct its business in the most profitable way for the greatest good of the greatest number of Americans.

Both in World War I and World War II, America entered late into the conflict. In fact, there were an enormous number of Americans, sometimes a majority, who had no interest whatever in participating in European wars. It was only after American ships were attacked in World War I and Pearl Harbor was attacked in World War II that America roused from its slumber and went to war. But when the war was over, the United States withdrew most of its troops, shut down its war machine, and went back to business.

America in the Twenty-First Century

This history is often forgotten or willfully ignored by dishonest politicians and journalists. Questioning Secretary of State Colin Powell in 2003, a television commentator demanded to know why it was that the United States was going to war in Afghanistan and Iraq and becoming an imperial power.

General Powell replied, referring to U.S. efforts in World War II, *"When all these conflicts were over, what did we do? Did we stay and conquer? Did we say 'Okay, we defeated Germany. Now Germany belongs to us? We defeated Japan, so Japan belongs to us?' No. What did we do? We built them up. We gave them democratic systems which they have embraced totally to their soul. And did we ask for any land? No, the only land we have ever asked for is enough land to bury our dead. And that is the kind of nation we are."*

Alone in the world, America remains the great power. In all of human history, America is the only country that has never expanded by using its military might to conquer and colonize other nations.

The Aims of American Diplomacy

The interests of America in foreign policy have almost always been the maintenance of relations with other nations that support the democratic, free enterprise business system. Foreign policy has always been aimed at creating or maintaining a situation in the world that assures a steady flow of imports, a steady market for exports, and a good climate for business.

George Washington once said, *"Nations have no friends, only interests."* All nations act in their own best interests. Politicians and diplomats of the United States are charged by the American people to make decisions and take actions that are in the best interests of the United States. To derogatorily accuse America of *acting in its own best interests* in foreign affairs suggests that the accuser is a very stupid person and completely ignorant of the way the world works.

The Rise and Fall of Empires
Historian Arnold Toynbee identified twenty-six large empires that had risen and fallen throughout history, beginning with the Persian Empire in 600 BC all the way through to the Japanese Empire which collapsed in 1945. The only one still standing was the American empire.

For most of history, well into the twentieth century and even the twenty-first century, tyrannies, dictatorships, megalomaniacs, and empires of all kinds have governed the world.

In most countries in the world today, especially in Africa, the Middle East, and South America, corruption, thievery, deceit, treachery, and murder are the normal state of affairs.

Most Americans living in "fortress America" do not realize that outside of the Western countries, which are largely governed by law, much of the world is governed by corrupt and dishonest dictators and politicians who lie, cheat, and steal continually.

A High Trust Nation
In America, integrity is highly respected and valued. It is demanded not only in positions of leadership but at all levels of society. According to Francis Fukuyama, in his bestselling book

Trust, America is one of the highest trusted nations in the world and in history.

Lying, cheating, and stealing are not acceptable in America and are both discouraged and punished, socially and legally. When it takes place, as in the corporate scandals following the 1990s boom, it is aggressively investigated and rooted out. The worst thing you can do to a public or private figure is to impugn his integrity, to suggest that he is dishonest in some way.

In other countries, there is much greater acceptance for or resignation about corruption in high places. For example, in the 2004 World Corruption Index, France came in at number eighteen, just below Botswana. Behaviors that are overlooked or ignored in France would lead to removal from office in the United States. This is true in many other countries as well.

To Protect and Defend

To preserve peace and stability in the world, and sometimes to achieve it, America has had no choice but to build powerful and far-reaching armed forces. Without the imposition of U.S. forces in Germany between 1945 and 1991, the U.S.S.R. would probably have overrun Western Europe. Without the presence of U.S. Forces in the Far East, the Mainland Chinese would have overrun Taiwan and Hong Kong. North Korea might have invaded South Korea again in the absence of American forces. Even the conflict in Vietnam was motivated by a desire to help an ally and defeat an enemy that was fully supported by Russia and Red China.

In every case, however well or poorly U.S. Forces have been deployed, the goal was always to achieve or maintain peace and world trade from which the people of the U.S., directly and indirectly, would benefit. In achieving these aims, the rest of the free world benefited as well.

Conflict in the Middle East

The United States produces about 30 percent of all the goods and services in the world with only 6 percent of its population. In order to support its massive industrial base, it requires energy of all kinds, including oil. Today, the U.S. imports about 53 percent of its oil needs, with fully 23 percent of that coming from the Middle East, especially Saudi Arabia.

Any curtailment of oil flow from the Middle East would deal a severe blow to the United States and to European economies, as well as to Japan and China.

For fifty years, the Middle East was left to itself. It consists of twenty-two impoverished states, all run by dictators and thugs and controlled by secret police. There exist no rights for women, no rights to property, no legal systems, and no safety or security for the average man or woman.

But as long as the oil continued to flow from the oil fields along the Persian Gulf, the problems in that area were not considered to be the business of America. It was not our job to interfere with the internal activities of sovereign nations in the Middle East.

Backward and Impoverished

Historically, the Middle East and the Arab nations have been some of the most backward and impoverished areas of the world. It was only when American entrepreneurs like J. Paul Getty invested enormous amounts of money searching for oil in Saudi Arabia that these countries had any source of wealth whatsoever. Today, aside from oil royalties and revenues, Finland, with one-fiftieth the population of the Middle East, exports more products than all the countries of the Middle East put together.

The dictatorships, despots, and royal families of Saudi Arabia,

Iraq, Iran, Abu Dhabi, Yemen, and each country where American or European companies have discovered oil have seized all of the oil riches in those countries. Overnight, they were infected with the *something for nothing* disease. From impoverished nomadic tribes, they suddenly became some of the richest people in the world. They eagerly divided this loot up amongst themselves, their families, and their close associates. But no amount was ever enough. No matter how much they got, they wanted and spent more and more.

Meanwhile, their populations languished in poverty in the one hundred degree-plus desert sun. Today, the populations of the Arab countries, even those with fabulous oil riches and countless tens of billions of dollars gushing into their bank accounts, are some of the most impoverished and wretched people on earth. Somehow, "trickle down" economics doesn't work in non-democratic societies.

Iraq and the Gulf

When Saddam Hussein and Iraq invaded Kuwait in 1990, with the primary aim of first of all wiping out tens of billions of dollars of debt, and second of all looting and plundering the oil-rich state, the situation in the Middle East changed dramatically and the United States had to intervene.

In conjunction with thirty other countries, including France and Germany, the U.S. mobilized its forces, drove the Iraqi army out of Kuwait, and defeated the fourth largest army in the world in a battle lasting 104 hours, with limited casualties on the U.S. side.

Then, consistent with decades of U.S. policy in the Middle East, with the job done, and Kuwait liberated, the U.S. military largely packed up and went home.

For the next ten years, Saddam Hussein defied U.N. resolutions and restrictions. He mass murdered more than 300,000 Shiites who disagreed with him and his Sunni supporters.

Year by year, he intensified his terrorization of his own people, brutally torturing and murdering thousands of men, woman, and children, while he plundered his own country. While his people suffered for lack of food and medicine, Saddam Hussein built dozens of massive palaces all over the country for himself and his family.

The Day the World Changed Forever

Then came 9/11. Suicidal, Islamist fanatics suddenly and brutally mass murdered almost 3000 Americans. Throughout the Middle East, people danced in the streets and cheered when they heard about the bombing of the Twin Trade Center Towers and the jet flying into the Pentagon. Fanatics proclaimed everywhere that this was the beginning of the war against "The Great Satan." On that day, the world changed forever.

The United States immediately mobilized its allies, swept into Afghanistan from all sides, and defeated the Taliban in less than a month, something the U.S.S.R. had been unable to accomplish in thirteen years and after suffering 50,000 casualties. Meanwhile, Saddam Hussein, who had almost built a nuclear reactor at Osirak some years before, continued to defy U.N. resolutions to disarm. In 1998, he ordered weapons inspectors out of Iraq and began acting in every way as if he had weapons of mass destruction to hide from Allied powers. He publicly gave $25,000 each to the families of suicide bombers in Israel, a U.S. ally, and hinted at further attacks on U.S. interests.

President George Bush, in his speech to Congress in 2003 said, *"The world's worst people must not be allowed to get control of the world's worst weapons."*

U.S. state policy, which had been reactive and defensive for 200 years, suddenly changed. Under President George Bush, the United States decided upon a doctrine of "preemption" for the first time in U.S. history. From then on, the U.S. would attack *first* if there was a possibility of an attack like 9/11 that would kill innocent Americans.

The Big Payoff

But Saddam Hussein was not stupid. For the twelve years since being defeated in the Gulf War, he had been forging economic ties with the French, Russians, Germans, and even the Chinese. He had promised the development of the Tikrit Oil Fields, containing seventeen trillion dollars worth of oil, to France if they would keep supporting his dictatorship and keep the Americans out of Iraq.

Records found in Baghdad after the 2003 Iraq war included a list of 270 people who had been bribed with Iraqi oil during the U.N. embargo, including the top people at the U.N. in charge of monitoring the embargo and the revenue flows. Initial estimates of the amounts stolen came to ten billion dollars. And this is probably just the tip of the iceberg. Politicians and businesspeople throughout Europe and the world turned out to have been on Saddam's payroll.

Something for nothing had struck again! The prospect of millions and billions of oil dollars flowing into Swiss accounts quickly got the French, German, Russian, and Belgians to link arms to block the U.S. invasion, but to no avail.

The purpose of invading Iraq was to rid the world of a murderous dictator who controlled unlimited billions of dollars and who was prepared to provide arms, money, and resources to terrorists who would strike America and Americans anywhere. The choice was simple. Either fight and defeat the terrorists in Iraq, or fight them in the streets of the United States. The U.S. decided to invade Iraq. It was the correct choice.

Leaders Must Lead

Many people don't understand the unique and special role of America in the world today. Either as the result of ignorance or cowardice, or both, they have become detached from reality.

Where did they ever get the idea that the United States could be the richest and most powerful country in the world without accepting the vast responsibilities that go along with that position of power?

Whoever said that America could have power, affluence, opportunity, and growth on the cheap, that we could achieve and maintain our greatness in the world at no cost?

The Bible says, *"From those to whom much has been given, much is expected."* The United States and the people of America are perhaps the most blessed in the world, and this means that we owe a lot. Much is expected from us. We have huge responsibilities.

There is no such thing as *something for nothing* in world affairs. The central responsibility of our leaders is to act in our best interests, to protect and preserve our *"inalienable rights to life, liberty, and the pursuit of happiness."*

No sane person wants war, with the suffering and death that war always entails. But no responsible leader can fail to act when the stakes are so high.

Why Do They Hate Us?

This question is repeated over and over by people who think that the most important goal America should have is to be *liked* by other countries. But the approval or disapproval of other countries can be extremely shallow. It blows in the wind. It comes and goes and changes like the weather. It is not reliable and therefore not particularly valuable in most cases.

First of all, most people in the world admire and look up to America and the American ideals of freedom, liberty, and opportunity. These are the dreams and hopes of all people everywhere, and America represents the highest expression of these ideals ever achieved by any nation in history.

Envy and Resentment Lurk Everywhere

But the twin emotions of *envy* and *resentment* lie just beneath the surface, waiting to be triggered by a person or event. In talking with people throughout Europe, Asia, and Australia, as well as all over America, you often hear them say, *"George Bush is dumb. George Bush is an out-of-control cowboy. George Bush is a warmonger. George Bush is controlled by a neo-con cabal, etc. etc."*

Since very few people think seriously or read extensively in these areas, when people holding these opinions are asked where they get their ideas, they ultimately refer to the newspapers and television programs.

Consider the Source

Where did these newspaper and television stories originate? It turns out that virtually every anti-American, anti-Bush story is an almost verbatim attack from Democratic partisans who are still angry about the fact that George Bush won the election for the presidency in 2000.

Fully 89 percent of newsmakers in radio, television, newspapers, and magazines identify themselves as Democratic supporters who dislike and disagree with Bush and the Republicans and have felt this way virtually all of their adult lives. Their anti-Bush accusations are therefore repeated over and over, until more and more people start to believe them. This is the standard use of the "big lie" theory, which says that if you repeat a lie often enough, in enough different forms, eventually a considerable number of people will begin to believe it.

The World Press

In Europe, many of the anti-American journalists and newsmakers were on the Iraqi payroll. Many of the sources of the news and newspaper stories, constantly attacking and belittling George Bush, turn out to be straight reprints in European newspapers from American newspapers. Democratic inspired attacks on Republicans and Bush are reprinted worldwide as if they were facts.

When people in Europe or Asia are told that George Bush is known to be an honest, intelligent, hard-working, non-drinking family man with degrees from both Harvard and Yale, they are astonished.

When they learn that fully 50 percent or more of Americans like and respect George Bush, their jaws drop. When George Bush won the 2004 presidential election by more than 3,000,000 votes, they were incredulous. They had been led to believe that he was extraordinarily unpopular in America.

The primary reason for this confusion is that what they, and Americans for that matter, read in the paper or hear on television is about 90 percent negative regarding George Bush and his administration.

When they are told about the intelligence, experience, qualities, and backgrounds of the senior policy makers in the Bush administration, they shake their heads. They had no idea. According to the stories in the American press, George Bush is an idiot, surrounded by incompetents, obsessed with projecting

American power in Iraq and throughout the world. When they learn that none of this is true, they often appear stunned.

No Principles Involved

The politics of France, Germany, and Russia toward America and Iraq have nothing whatever to do with values or principles. They are driven completely by the desire to get or keep *something for nothing.* They are motivated by the E-Factor and obsessed with getting or keeping the power and money that goes with their positions.

In terms of defense, the French, Germans, and Russians have cut back on military spending year after year. Their armies are poorly trained and equipped. When they say that they will not support an American action in Iraq, much of the reason is because they have nothing to support it with. They are over-regulated, over-taxed, over-tired, and incapable of playing a role in the world.

The bottom line in foreign policy is this. True friendships with other countries, such as America has with Tony Blair in England, with John Howard in Australia, and with the leaders of the thirty or more other countries who support the United States in Iraq, are only really tested *under fire*, when major issues are at stake.

The idea that "we need our allies" is simply not true. We do not need to compromise our safety or our ideals in order to earn the support or approval of people who stab us in the back as soon as they are offered a bigger personal payout from someone like Saddam Hussein. Fair-weather friends are not worth having or working for.

They will let us down again and again whenever the going gets tough or whenever they see it in their best interests to do so. As politicians, they are totally expedient in every way, completely divorced from any values or principles whatever.

Economically, these countries that make every attempt to undermine and hurt us will continue to trade with us as long as it is expedient, almost as if economic relations take place on another plane, in another dimension of space.

What about the United Nations?

Virtually everyone wants to help the less fortunate. We are strongly moved by stories and pictures of hunger, disease, famine, and deprivation in other parts of the world. We want someone to do something about it, to alleviate these tragic situations. We therefore give our support to organizations that promise to alleviate suffering that we can personally do nothing about. This is the primary role of the United Nations.

In addition, everyone wants *peace*. There is a natural revulsion to wars, conflicts, and the deaths and suffering that they entail. No intelligent person wants war of any kind. Most efforts by diplomats and politicians on the world stage are aimed at creating and maintaining conditions of peaceful trade and cooperation that are conducive to the greatest good for the greatest number of people. This universal desire was the motivating force for the establishment of the United Nations after World War II.

The Great Failure

The United Nations is largely a *failure* in achieving either of these two noble goals. It has become a den of thieves and corruption, staffed by incompetent, dishonest, over-paid people whose primary aim in life is to get *something for nothing*, for themselves, their friends, their associates, and their countries.

The United Nations has a virtually unbroken record of incompetence, clumsiness, inefficiency, and corruption in virtually everything it has ever attempted to do. It has never solved a major human problem, stopped or prevented a war or conflict, or even enforced any of its resolutions, in spite of the countless billions of dollars that have disappeared down its drain in the name of worthy causes.

Expediency Run Wild

Every person with a position at the United Nations is *lazy, greedy, ambitious, selfish, vain, ignorant, and impatient,* motivated to get *safety, security, comfort, leisure, love, respect, and fulfillment,* with a special focus on *power* and *money,* and completely unconcerned about the long-term consequences of their actions or inactions. Each of them continually strives for the six P's: *paychecks, perks, position, power, privileges, and pensions.*

The United States pays 22 percent of the costs of the United Nations, and aside from having one vote on the fifteen-member Security Council, it only has one vote out of 194 countries represented. These countries continuously outvote the U.S. and override virtually every American position. Last year, they voted the United States off the Committee for Human Rights and made Libya, one of the worst human-rights violators in the world, the senior country in charge.

No Intelligent Purpose

The United Nations is a sounding board for despotic countries that manipulate its activities and sell their votes behind the scenes in exchange for monies deposited into their Swiss bank accounts.

U.N. diplomats and staff live like kings everywhere they go. In the process of politicking and pontificating, they fly first class, stay at the best hotels, dine in the finest restaurants, and live in beautiful homes and apartments in some of the great cities of the world.

They pay no taxes and cannot be arrested for crimes, or even given parking tickets. They have "diplomatic immunity."

United Nations officials are appointed politically and owe no allegiance to anyone except the person who determines whether or not they keep their job.

They attend endless meetings whenever they feel like it, cast meaningless votes on unenforceable resolutions, and accomplish nothing.

If the U.N. did not exist today and someone proposed it, knowing what they now know, it would never be approved or supported, except by the parasites and bottom feeders who profit from its activities.

Anyone who looks to the U.N. for anything of any value is either ignorant of the complete dishonesty and uselessness of it or is totally blinded by the high-minded intentions of the organization in spite of sixty years of failure to the contrary.

The U.S. Must Stay the Course

Meanwhile, the United States must do what she feels is the right thing and stay the course. Other countries will either support us or not. Because of our desire to be liked, America has poured billions of dollars each year, totaling more than five trillion dollars already, into foreign aid to help these countries become more prosperous and democratic.

Even though these countries vote against us in the United Nations, do everything possible to undermine our national purposes, and desert us when we ask for their support and friendship, the United States continues to send them billions of dollars of *free money*. They have learned over time that there is no penalty for anything they do to harm American interests.

The U.S. plays a unique role in the world today. Alone amongst all nations with its power, the United States must embrace the responsibility of assisting and protecting an ungrateful world. The government of the United States must continue to do everything possible to fight for and maintain an America that is good and beneficial for the greatest number of Americans.

America and Americans have been entrusted with guarding and preserving the American Dream, not only for ourselves but for all of mankind. We must maintain America as "the last, best hope of mankind," so she will always be seen as "the shining city upon a hill." This is America's destiny.

"Do not pray for tasks equal to your powers; pray for powers equal to your tasks."

— Phillips Brooks

"Nothing splendid has ever been achieved except by those who dared believe that something inside of them was superior to circumstance."

— Bruce Barton

The great dilemma of our time is the growing obsession that so many people have to get *something for nothing*. It is bankrupting our society and the societies of every nation that has embraced the idea of *free money*. The idea of being able to bribe people with their own money and then put the burden of repayment onto unborn generations pits everyone against everyone, turning ordinary people into mean, vicious, demanding, and dishonest claimants to money they have not earned and do not deserve.

Because we have spent so many years creating this situation of national insolvency, the solutions to our problems will be painful and difficult. But the starting point is to admit that this national and worldwide obsession to get *something for nothing* cannot endure. At the end of this road, if we do not turn back, lies economic and social collapse and bankruptcy. Fortunately, it is not too late.

What To Do Now

First and foremost, each person must accept responsibility for himself, and then for America and the future. No one may stand aside and blame the situation on others. That path leads to hopelessness, victimhood, and abdication of personal accountability.

Second, we must slam the door on any further *something for nothing* programs or proposals. We should only spend money that we have. Every plan to spend any money from the taxpay-

243

ers and the public purse must be paid for in full, in advance. We must never again commit *free money* to anyone that is to be paid at a later time. If we do not have the money, we do not spend it. Period.

Third, we must assume from the beginning that every action is motivated by the desire to get *something for nothing*, and we should put the onus on any politician or activist to prove beyond a questionable doubt that he is not simply *lazy, greedy, ambitious, selfish, vain, ignorant, and impatient*, motivated by the desire to get *safety, security, comfort, leisure, love, respect, and fulfillment* for himself the fastest and easiest way possible, with little concern for the long term consequences of his actions.

Fourth, we should go back through every public policy and program and ruthlessly weed out every *something for nothing* scheme that gives free money to anyone for any reason. We should restructure every welfare program so that recipients are required to earn the money in some way.

Fifth, we should not allow anyone to get the things he wants except by engaging in behaviors based on voluntary cooperation that benefit and enhance both the individual and all others who are affected.

Sixth, we must encourage a new birth of prosperity by altering or eliminating every law that hinders the entrepreneurial instincts and innovations that create hope, jobs, and opportunities for more people. We must commit to making and maintaining the United States as the most vibrant entrepreneurial democracy in the world.

Finally, the seventh prescription is that we once again commit to the American Dream of freedom in all areas, of *equality* before the law, especially in the areas of taxes and enterprise, *personal responsibility* for everything one does and becomes, *self-reliance* as the basis of personal pride and dignity, and *limited government,* which is vital to assure all the other benefits we desire.

The road ahead will not be easy, but it is within our abilities to achieve any goal, overcome any obstacle, and solve any problem we face. This is the essence of America, the "can do!" spirit. There are no limits except the ones we place on our own imaginations.

What is necessary, more than anything else, is "the will to do it."

About the Author

Brian Tracy is the top sales trainer in the world today and has trained more than one million salespeople in over 70 countries worldwide. He is the bestselling author of *Advanced Selling Strategies*, *The Psychology of Selling*, *Unlimited Sales Success*, and *Speak to Win*—plus over 60 other books. Brian has written and produced more than 500 audio and video learning programs on sales, management, success, business, and entrepreneurship. He is the president of Brian Tracy International, and Business Growth Strategies, an Internet-based company that helps businesses of all sizes increase their sales and profitability by implementing the best practices of top businesses worldwide.

THOMAS NELSON
Since 1798

Titles that Explore the Political Landscape
with Audacity and Integrity

CLEANING UP
One Man's Redemptive Journey through
the Seductive World of Corporate Crime
By Barry Minkow
1-5955-5004-6

In this eye-opening book, Barry Minkow, the one-time Wall Street wiz kid who rocked the financial world with one of its biggest scams, tells the riveting true story of how he turned from con to cop, turning his skills to outing crooks and investment scams, and even training FBI agents to do the same. Part autobiography, part exposé, and part wake-up call, *Cleaning Up* is a fast-paced trip into the world of corporate crime, investment scams, pyramid schemes, and accounting fraud where billions of dollars is at stake. It follows Minkow through his multimillion dollar scheme, his stay in prison, and the life-changing events that followed.

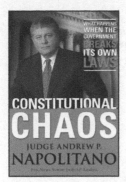

CONSTITUTIONAL CHAOS
*What Happens When the Government Breaks
Its Own Laws*
By Judge Andrew P. Napolitano
0-7852-6083-8

In this alarming book, Fox News commentator Judge Napolitano makes the solid case that there is a pernicious and ever-expanding pattern of government abuse in America's criminal justice system, leading him to establish his general creed: "The government is not your friend." As an attorney, a law professor, a commentator, a judge, and now a successful television personality, Judge Napolitano has studied the system inside and out, and his unique voice has resonance and relevance. Napolitano sets the record straight, speaking frankly from his own experiences and investigation about how government agencies will often arrest without warrant, spy without legal authority, imprison without charge, and kill without cause.

SIZE MATTERS
*How Big Government Puts the Squeeze on
America's Families, Finances, and Freedom*
By Joel Miller
1-5955-5037-2

The federal government has seventeen million employees, an annual budget of $2.5 trillion, and heaps up thousands of pages worth of new regulations every year. This continually swelling government is squeezing entrepreneurs, workers, and families in ways that reduce wealth, hurt finances, and constrict our lives. Using studies about economic freedom and the near endless extent of government regulation, along with vivid anecdotes of individuals struggling to make it in an environment where the state hampers their lifestyle and liberty, Joel Miller reveals the real daily drawbacks of Big Government and the outlook for turning things around.

SPYCHIPS
How Major Corporations and Government Plan to Track Your Every Move with RFID
By Katherine Albrecht and Liz McIntyre
1-5955-5020-8

RFID, which stands for Radio Frequency IDentification, is a technology that uses computer chips smaller than a grain of sand to track items from a distance. And as this mind-blowing book explains, plans and efforts are being made now by global corporations and the U.S government to turn this advanced technology, these spychips, into a way to track our daily activities—and keep us all on Big Brother's short leash. Compiling massive amounts of research with firsthand knowledge, *Spychips* explains RFID technology and reveals the history and future of the master planners' strategies to imbed these trackers on everything—from postage stamps to shoes to people themselves—and spy on Americans without our knowledge or consent.

A JEALOUS GOD
Science's Crusade against Religion
By Pamela R. Winnick
1-5955-5019-4

In this riveting and alarming book, award-winning journalist Pamela R. Winnick reveals the many ways in which science has eroded human dignity and shielded itself from scrutiny by attacking religion—becoming itself an oppressive, narrow-minded system of faith that blindly pursues its own dangerous objectives, shirking off traditional values and moral responsibilities. Covering the history and current politics of today's hot-button topics—stem cell research, cloning, intelligent design, and more—former medical reporter Winnick shows that, in today's upside-down world of mathematical absolutes and moral relativism, science has veered off course and endangers us all.

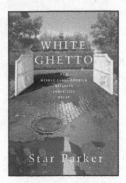

WHITE GHETTO
How Middle Class America Reflects the Decay of the Inner City
By Star Parker
1-5955-5027-5

In this provocative book, spitfire Star Parker proves that urban plight simply reveals a decay that is gnawing its way throughout American society as a whole. The sexual chaos, values disorientation, and social turmoil we see in our inner cities, Parker contends, is merely a more sharply focused picture of moral collapse in mainstream America. Covering today's biggest social issues, Parker argues that wealth and infrastructure have cushioned the collapse in the 'burbs but the disease is the same and only waits for the support structures to falter and fracture before ghetto culture hits the family down the street, or in your own house.

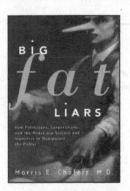

BIG FAT LIARS
How Politicians, Corporations, and the Media Use Science and Statistics to Manipulate the Public
By Morris E. Chafetz M.D.
1-5955-5008-9

Morris Chafetz, president of the Health Education Foundation, has spent decades carefully observing trends in science, government, the legal system, and the media, and now he reveals his unexpected findings in this sharp exposé of the many statistical lies— lies about everything from terrorism to the environment to alcohol and tobacco addiction—that manipulate Americans for the sinister motives of government, the media, corporations, and meretricious lawyers. Clear-sighted and far-reaching, this book will change how you look and listen to the scads of stats that are thrust on us every day.

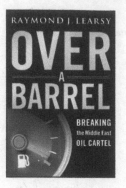

OVER A BARREL
Breaking the Middle East Oil Cartel
By Raymond J. Learsy
1-5955-5036-4

Longtime commodities trader Raymond J. Learsy lifts the veil of the Mideast oil cartel, showing how OPEC manipulates the oil markets and destabilizes the world's economy by twisting bogus perceptions of oil scarcity to hike prices and gain political power; using Islamist terrorist connections that fuel anti-American hatreds with dollars from our own wallets; keeping Third-World nations in abject poverty despite their rich oil deposits; and becoming the de facto master of Iraq's newly liberated oil fields. A sharp, sweeping survey of OPEC's methods of economic dominance, this book explains how to bust the Mideast oil cartel and chart our own course toward energy independence.

TAX REVOLT
The Rebellion against an Overbearing, Bloated, Arrogant, and Abusive Government
By Phil Valentine
1-5955-5001-1

This book is the powerful rallying cry to all Americans to continue to fight against our ever-increasing taxes. Taking a close look at the heroic incident in Tennessee, when citizens converged on the state capitol to protest and repeatedly beat back attempts to pass a state tax, Valentine weaves an inspiring story of how patriotic citizens have stood up to taxes in the past, how many intrepid constituents continue to fight, and how Americans should resist and even revolt against taxes on a state and national level.

THOMAS NELSON
Since 1798

What people are saying about Thomas Nelson books:

BILL O'REILLY
about Judge Andrew P. Napolitano's *Constitutional Chaos*
"This book will open your eyes."

ANN COULTER
about Richard Poe's *Hillary's Secret War*
"This book is required reading."

SEAN HANNITY
about Jesse Lee Peterson's *Scam*
"[A] bold prescription to make America a better place."

RUSH LIMBAUGH
about Star Parker's *Uncle Sam's Plantation*
"[This book] casts new light on the redemptive power of freedom."

GLENN BECK
about Jayna Davis's *The Third Terrorist*
"When you read this book, you are going to be convinced
that it is the truth."

SAM DONALDSON
about John McCaslin's *Inside the Beltway*
"Whether you are a Democrat or a Republican,
you will love this book."

NEIL CAVUTO
about Barry Minkow's *Cleaning Up*
"[This] one-of-a-kind story makes for indispensable reading."

GEORGE WILL
about Craig Shirley's *Reagan's Revolution*
"This is an exhilarating story of political daring."

HUGH HEWITT
about Ben Shapiro's *Brainwashed*
"A brilliant new voice for a generation of activists."

MICHAEL MEDVED
about Rebecca Hagelin's *Home Invasion*
"[O]ffers a persuasive, common-sense voice that
demands respect-and attention ... "

ROBERT D. NOVAK
about Tom Coburn's *Breach of Trust*
"This book provides a rare, invaluable portrait of life as it
really is on Capitol Hill ..."